Prayers for a New World

PRAYERS FOR
A NEW WORLD

Compiled and Edited by

JOHN WALLACE SUTER

Charles Scribner's Sons · New York

Acknowledgments

The Editor extends his thanks to the friends who over the years have shared with him prayers they have written for their own use in private, or in the family, or for a parish bulletin. Some asked to remain anonymous. All were moved by the generous thought that their contributions might be of help, as indeed they were. Any of these friends who read this paragraph will know that it was written for them, as an expression of sincere gratitude.

Publishers and individuals who have allowed the Editor to make use of copyright material are listed below, with thanks not only for permissions graciously given, but more especially for their friendly and constructive interest in the gradual assembly of the prayers which constitute this book. Some of the material, drawn from prayers which originated many years or centuries ago, are in the public domain. Further information may be found in the list of Sources.

Abington Press:
  Lift Up your Hearts by Walter Russell Bowie. Copyright © 1939, 1956 by Pierce & Washabaugh. *A Private House of Prayer*. Copyright © 1958 by Leslie D. Weatherhead. *A Book of Pastoral Prayers* by Ernest Fremont Tittle. Copyright 1951 by Pierce & Smith.
Association Press:
  The Willow and the Bridge by Toyohiko Kagawa and Franklin Cole.
George Allen & Unwin Ltd.:
  Litany of Remembrance by Bishop George Ridding.
Bruce Barton and The Bobbs Merrill Company:
  The Soul of Abraham Lincoln by William E. Barton. Also reprinted from *The Religion of Abraham Lincoln* © 1959 and 1963 by William J. Wolf, The Seabury Press, Publishers. The first edition, published in 1959 by Doubleday & Co., Inc., carried the title: *The Almost Chosen People*.
Barton, Mayhew & Co., London:
  The Old World and the New by L. H. M. Soulsby (published by Longmans, Green & Co. Limited).
Board of Publication, The United Lutheran Church in America:
  Collects and Prayers. Edited by The Common Service Book Committee. 1935.

The Fortress Press (formerly The Muhlenberg Press):
Prayers of the Reformers, edited by Clyde Manschreck.

The British Broadcasting Corporation:
Services for Broadcasting.

Curtis Brown, Ltd.:
A Thomas Merton Reader edited by Thomas P. McDonnell.

Rev. Charles H. Buck, Jr., Dean of St. Paul's Cathedral, Boston, Mass.:
Prayers in many booklets compiled and edited by the late Dean Edmund S. Rousmaniere. Used by permission.

Burns & Oates, Ltd.:
The Psalms trans. by Ronald Knox.

Cambridge University Press, London:
The Scottish Book of Common Prayer.

Central Board of Finance, Church of England:
A prayer from The Book of Common Prayer Proposed in 1928; with the permission of the holders of the copyright.

Challenge Books & Pictures, London:
A Book of Prayers Written for Use in an Indian College by J. S. Hoyland.

The Church Pension Fund:
Prayer Book Studies XVI

Church Society for College Work:
A prayer by Gregory Vlastos who also graciously gives permission for its use.

J. M. Dent & Sons Ltd:
Devotional Services for Public Worship by John Hunter.

Dodd, Mead & Company:
A Book of Prayers by Samuel McComb.

E. P. Dutton & Co., Inc.:
Devotional Services for Public Worship by John Hunter.

Episcopal Pacifist Fellowship: For a prayer prepared by them.

Friends Home Service Committee, London:
A Day-Book of Counsel and Comfort, from the Epistles of George Fox. Compiled by L. Violet Hodgkin. 1937.

The General Synod of the Church of Ireland:
The Book of Common Prayer of the Church of Scotland.

Groton School:
Prayers Used at Groton School, privately printed.

Harcourt, Brace & World, Inc.:
A Thomas Merton Reader edited by Thomas P. McDonnell. © 1962 by The Abbey of Gethsemani, Inc.

Harper & Row, Publishers, Inc.:
Draw Near with Faith by S. S. Drury; *A Book of Public Prayer* by Harry Emerson Fosdick; *The Book of English Collects* edited by John

W. Suter; *Prayers of the Spirit* by John W. Suter; *Prayers for Daily Services* by Samuel H. Miller.

Hodder & Stoughton, Ltd.:
The Epistle to the Hebrews trans. by William Manson.

Holt, Rinehart and Winston, Inc.:
"They Say in the Colleges" by McGeorge Bundy, contained in *Zero Hour: A Summons to the Free*.

The Indian Society for Promoting Christian Knowledge, Delhi, India:
The Book of Common Prayer (1960) of the Church of India, Pakistan, Burma, and Ceylon. With the consent of His Grace the Metropolitan, the Most Rev. Hiyanirindu Lakdasa Jacob de Mel.

Longmans, Green & Co. Limited:
Prayers for the City of God by Gilbert C. Binyon; *An Anthology of Prayers* by A. S. T. Fisher.

The Macmillan Company:
The Art of Ministering to the Sick by Richard C. Cabot and Russell L. Dicks; *Christ's Victory and Ours* by Frederick C. Grant.

The Manuscript Division of The Library of Congress:
In whose custody are "The Bishop Charles Henry Brent Papers."

Morehouse-Barlow Co., Inc.:
The Prayer Manual by Frederick B. Mcnutt; *After the Third Collect* by E. Milner-White; *A Century of Collects* edited by Atwell M. Y. Baylay for the Alcuin Club; prayers by Francis C. Lightbourn, published in *The Living Church*; *A Book of Collects* by "Pater and Filius" (Morehouse Publishing Co., Milwaukee, 1919).

A. R. Mowbray & Co., Ltd.:
After the Third Collect by E. Milner-White; *The Prayer Manual* by Frederick B. Mcnutt; *The Church in Germany in Prayer* by Walter Kagerah and Robert A. S. Martineau; *A Nation at Prayer* by W. B. Trevelyan; *The Mantle of Prayer* by Gina Harwood and Arthur W. Hopkinson; *Sons of God*.

Oxford University Press, New York:
The Kingdom, the Power and the Glory (The Grey Book, copyright 1933 by Oxford and 1961 by Bradford Young); *The Pastor's Prayerbook* by Robert N. Rodenmayer; *The Oxford American Prayer Book Commentary* by Massey H. Shepherd, Jr.; *Prayers of the Christian Life* by John Underwood Stephens. Copyright © 1952 by Oxford University Inc.

Oxford University Press, London:
The Proposed Prayer Book of the Church of England 1928; *The 1960 Book of Common Prayer of the Church of the Province of South Africa*; *Book of Common Order*, Church of Scotland; *Prayers for the Christian Year* by permission of the Committee on Public Worship and Aids to Devotion of the General Assembly of the Church of Scotland, and Oxford University Press; *Daily Prayer* by Eric Milner-White

and G. W. Briggs; *The Daily Service* by G. W. Briggs; *The Kingdom, the Power and the Glory,* American edition of *The Grey Book; A Diary of Private Prayer* by John Baillie.

William Scarlett:

To Will One Thing, privately printed.

Charles Scribner's Sons:

A Diary of Private Prayer by John Baillie. Copyright 1949 Charles Scribner's Sons. *Joy in Believing, Selections from the Written Words and Prayers of Henry Sloane Coffin,* edited by Walter Russell Bowie. Copyright © 1956 Dorothy Prentice Coffin. *Youth Talks with God,* by Avery Brooke. Copyright © 1959 Avery Brooke. *Pastoral Prayers Through the Year,* compiled by Robert L. Eddy. Copyright © 1959 Robert L. Eddy. *Prayers for Services,* compiled by Morgan Phelps Noyes. Copyright 1934 Charles Scribner's Sons. *Prayers Written at Vailima* by Robert Louis Stevenson.

The Seabury Press:

Key Words for Lent by George W. Barrett, © 1963 by The Seabury Press, Inc., New York; *A Boy's Prayer Book* compiled by J. W. Suter. © 1957 by The Seabury Press, Inc., New York; *By Means of Death* by Hughell E. W. Fosbroke, © 1956 by The Seabury Press, Inc., New York; *Book of Prayer for Everyman* by Theodore Parker Ferris, © 1962 by The Seabury Press, Inc., New York; *A Manual of Eastern Orthodox Prayers.* Published for the Fellowship of St Alban and St Sergius.

Sheed & Ward Inc., New York:

The Psalms trans. by Ronald Knox; The Scripture quotations are in the translation of Monsignor Knox, Copyright 1944, 1948 and 1950 by Sheed & Ward Inc., New York. With the kind permission of the Archbishop of Westminster.

The Society for Promoting Christian Knowledge, London:

A Manual of Eastern Orthodox Prayers. Published for the Fellowship of St Alban and St Sergius; *Service Book for Youth* by S. M. Trood.

Student Christian Movement Press Limited:

A Book of Prayers for Schools edited by Hugh Martin; *A Book of Prayers for Students.*

The University of Chicago Press:

The Prayers of Kierkegaard edited by Perry D. LeFevre, © 1956 by The University of Chicago.

The Westminster Press:

The Book of Common Worship, copyright 1946, The Board of Christian Education Presbyterian Church U.S.A.; *Prayers for Church Workers* edited by Kendig Brubacker Cully. Copyright © 1961 by W. L. Jenkins.

Foreword

This book of prayers has three purposes in its immediate favor. It is historical. In one volume Dr. Suter has compiled triumphant Christian prayers of the ages. It is comprehensive. From Quaker to Catholic, the Christian prayer life of the world is reflected in this book. It is personal. Within moments of perusal you will find "your prayer", and share it with others.

These are the first impressions we receive as we read *Prayers For a New World*. Then we find other treasures. We need the best prayers inspired by God for the peace of the world and they are here generously provided. We all desire deeper encounters with God and the means are found in meditations and litanies. When our years increase and age tells its story we need prayers that have passed the test of time. They are here. When death moves close to us and our loved ones, we want confidence that cannot be shaken. It is given here in prayers that continue triumphantly through the centuries.

William Temple said, "No man can be fully appreciated by those who do not know him personally." As one who has known Dr. Suter for many years I am constantly inspired by his prayer life. All of us who treasure his friendship "fully appreciate" his Christian insight. But it is simply impossible for us to know the saints and prophets who have written the prayers in this book. Many of them lived centuries ago and others who are still living may be in far away places. Dr. Suter has a special grace which enables him in prayer to penetrate both time and distance. He knows the authors of these prayers personally, in spirit. And that can be more creative than a few years spent with them in friendship. Through Dr. Suter's choice and arrangement of these prayers all of us will "fully appreciate" the souls who received and gave them.

Prayers For a New World provides a vast sweep of prayer life from the first days of our faith to these immediate moments of the twentieth century. This book will enter countless homes where faith is strong or weak and those who use it prayerfully will find a new world for themselves and others.

Charles Francis Hall, D.D.
Bishop of New Hampshire

Easter, 1964

The Art of Compiling

One purpose of this book is to set before the reader prayers which represent many types and many points-of-view. No attempt has been made to favor one over another. Let the prayers speak for themselves. I have tried to assemble specimens each of which is good of its kind.

Another aim, as the title implies, has been to select prayers appropriate for the new world which we have entered, where strenuous re-thinking is in order. The eternal truths are still eternally true, but our interpretations of them must move forward with the times and speak to current needs.

For more than thirty years I have been collecting prayers, and compilations of prayers. Some of the books were privately printed. A number of the prayers are in manuscript. Some address God as You instead of Thou. Through certain prayers there shines a glint of humor.

No other influence is as strong or pervasive as that of the Bible. When a direct quotation is used, this is obvious. More often, however, the influence is felt in paraphrase—either transparent, or so far removed from its origin as to be discernible only by one familiar with the source. The collect for the Sunday before Lent (page 122 in the American Prayer Book) could not have been written without knowledge of St. Paul's First Corinthians 13; nor prayer #219 in the present book without acquaintance with both Paul's letter and the Prayer Book's collect.

A typical compilation draws its material from sources which vary widely, both as to the times when they were written and in the religious convictions of the authors. But it is not only between the covers of a book that one finds variety. Equally striking are the variations among the compilers themselves in their treatments of the same material. Each has his personal method of selecting, and his manner of shaping and re-shaping what he selects. Indeed, every collection of prayers represents the confluence of the thoughts of the original authors (who are not always identified) and the use made of these thoughts by the compiler. The latter may adapt material to fit a need he has in mind, knowing that a change in wording can render it effective for his purpose without injury either to its central thought or to its style. Thus it is that Bishop Brent's prayer for a boys' school, shorn of the words applicable only to a school, becomes a general prayer on the theme of the higher patriotism (#40).

ADAPTATIONS

Among literary forms the prayer is unique in that it is written not simply to be read, like a poem or essay or novel, but to be *prayed*. This accounts for the many adaptations, abbreviations, and other changes one finds in all compilations. Dean Milner-White of York says that all modern editors adapt or abbreviate the prayers of England, adding, "Our forefathers were somewhat long-winded." Other compilers have noted that sometimes a passage which is not a prayer can be fashioned into one by changes that are mostly grammatical. Archaic phrases can be replaced by words more readily understood. Occasionally an editor will make alterations so extensive as to produce what is virtually a new prayer. If he is conscientious he acknowledges the source of his inspiration and takes full responsibility for the result. Most important of all is the need to subject some prayers to drastic revision, or even to omit them, because they strike a note that has become meaningless in the everyday lives of the people of our time. Nor need an author disdain to re-write his own prayers, as Bishop Brent so often did, and as I have done with many prayers taken from *Prayers of the Spirit*.

On the other hand it is a joy to take a magnificent prayer like James Martineau's (#173), and another from *The Book Annexed* (#37), and restore them to the original depth of thought and purity of design which many editorial hands had all but obliterated. Even the most fastidious editor-compiler will make some mistakes, injuring what he meant to improve, whether it be another's prayer or his own. Prayer composing is a fluid, flexible, and dangerous art. Dean Milner-White, speaking of a book he admires, says that though its prayers are too long, their manner and matter are excellent, "and extraction is not difficult." Not, perhaps, difficult for him; but for most, to be undertaken with caution.

Besides adapting, there is a considerable amount of borrowing. A phrase like "the swift and solemn trust of life", or "the royalty of inward happiness", tends to linger in the memory long after its source has been forgotten. One may therefore find it embodied in a prayer without any acknowledgment to Dr. Martineau or to L. H. M. Soulsby. Many a prayer begins with "O God, our help in ages past", with no recognition of either Isaac Watts or Psalm 90. Yet if every quotation and near-quotation were used "by permission" a compilation might have to devote as much space to notes as to prayers. Sometimes what is copyrighted in a collection of prayers is chiefly the book's arrangement and organization, its explanatory notes, an essay, a preface, indexes, and other items of like nature. To certain prayers, on the other hand, a publisher has exclusive rights.

"UNKNOWN"

Consider the various meanings attached to the familiar word "unknown". It can mean: That the prayer was thus labelled in the book where the compiler found it. That it is the result of a series of committee-meetings and no one person can be said to have written it. That the author asked to be anonymous. That the book it was found in gives no clue. Of course in the case of official Prayer Books, where many prayers are centuries old, the translator is more likely to be known than the author. To trace the lineage of such a prayer from book to book, language to language, and century to century, would require an extent and depth of research far beyond the range of the present book. Even the most learned and skilled researcher often finds the stream of such detailed history disappearing under ground.

ARCHAISMS AND MYSTERIES

Archaisms have their place. Indeed, the definition of the word is "ancient, old-fashioned, has ceased to be used except in poetry or church ritual." But it is important to understand their place in prayers. No archaism should be used if it seriously obscures the meaning of a sentence, least of all if it conveys a meaning contrary to the intention of the author. For example, in earlier days *suffer* meant *allow* or *let*; and *let* often meant *hinder*. Could anything be more confusing? However, an archaic word or phrase which causes no confusion as to its meaning may well be retained for its flavor or charm. To displace *Dearly beloved brethren* with *Dear brothers* would be of no help. Nor does it add clarity to substitute perfectly understandable prose for perfectly understandable poetry. "The wind bloweth where it listeth, and thou hearest the sound thereof, but canst not tell whence it cometh, and whither it goeth" is as easy to understand as The New English Bible's "The wind blows where it wills; you hear the sound of it, but you do not know where it comes from, or where it is going." In the writing of prayers there is room for poetic expression which does not obscure the meaning (#236).

MYSTERIES

Mystery also has its place. But here again we must make a distinction. The being of God no human mind can fully understand. Nobody will ever imprison God in a neat formula or exhaust the subject in a creed. The peace of God, as the benediction says, passeth (surpasses) all understanding. But statements which are beyond understanding only because they lack lucidity and precision denote fuzzy-mindedness and do not deserve the name mystery. The men who edited the first American Prayer Book in 1789 were aware of this when they put in their Preface the warning that a Prayer Book must speak in "the clearest, plainest, most affecting and majestic manner." This remarkable quartet of adjectives covers the essentials— understandability, beauty, mystery—and sets the high standard of excellence which prayer-writing deserves.

JOHN WALLACE SUTER

Contents

1 World Peace

2 *The Higher Patriotism*

3 *Intercessions*

4 *The Church*

5 *Ministers of Christ*

6 *Scholars*

7 *The Bible*

10   True Christian Graces

11 *Praise and Thanksgiving*

12 *The Life of Prayer*

13 *Self-Examination*

14 *Inner Peace*

15   Around the Clock

16   Milestones in the Christian Year

Christmastide

The New Year

Lent

Holy Week

Words From The Cross

Eastertide and the Ascension

Whitsuntide

17 Affirmations of Faith

18 The Ageing

19 *Sickness and Health*

20 *For the Dying*

21 *For the Departed and the Bereaved*

22 *Benedictions*

Prayers for a New World

1

World Peace

ALL THE SONS OF MEN °1

Remember in thy mercy, O God, all the sons of men. Let the whole earth be filled with thy praise and made glad by the knowledge of thy Name. May there fall upon all mankind a sense of thine excellent greatness. Let thy glory rule over every court and market-place, thy law be honored in every home. Redeem the whole world's life, O God, and transform it utterly, through the power of the Holy Cross.

JOHN BAILLIE

THAT PROMISED PEACE 2

O victorious Christ, whose redeeming love destroys the power of darkness and death and sin: Take thy place, we pray thee, upon the throne of our hearts; and so rule our lives by the might of thy Spirit wherewith we become free indeed, that through us and thy Church all peoples may come to that promised peace wherein nation shall not lift up sword against nation, neither learn war any more.

EPISCOPAL PACIFIST FELLOWSHIP

°This symbol (°) as it appears throughout the book indicates that the editor has commented on this prayer in the notes found on pages 219-226.

PRAYER FOR PEACE   °3

Almighty and merciful God, Father of all men, Creator and
      Ruler of the Universe,
Lord of History, whose designs are inscrutable, whose glory is
      without blemish, whose compassion for the errors of men
      is inexhaustible; in your will is our peace!

Mercifully hear this prayer which rises to you from the tumult
      and desperation of a world in which you are forgotten, in
      which your name is not invoked, your laws are derided, and
      your presence is ignored.
Because we do not know you, we have no peace.

From the heart of an eternal silence, you have watched the rise
      of empires and have seen the smoke of their downfall.

You have seen Egypt, Assyria, Babylon, Greece, and Rome,
      once powerful, carried away like sand in the wind.

You have witnessed the impious fury of ten thousand fratri-
      cidal wars, in which great powers have torn whole conti-
      nents to shreds in the name of peace and justice.

And now our nation itself stands in imminent danger of a war
      the like of which has never been seen!
This nation, dedicated to freedom, not to power,
Has obtained through freedom a power it did not desire.

And seeking by that power to defend its freedom, it is enslaved
      by the processes and policies of power.
Must we wage a war we do not desire, a war that can do us no
      good,
And which our very hatred of war forces us to prepare?

A day of ominous decision has now dawned on this free nation.
Armed with a titanic weapon, and convinced of our own right,
      we face a powerful adversary armed with the same weapon,
      equally convinced that he is right.

In this moment of destiny, this moment we never foresaw, we
    cannot afford to fail.
Our choice of peace or war may decide our judgment, and pub-
    lish it in an eternal record.

In this fatal moment of choice in which we might begin the
    patient architecture of peace,
We may also take the last step across the rim of chaos.

Save us then from our obsessions! Open our eyes, dissipate our
    confusions, teach us to understand ourselves and our
    adversary!
Let us never forget that sins against the law of love are pun-
    ished by loss of faith,
And those without faith stop at no crime to achieve their ends!

Help us to be masters of the weapons that threaten to master
    us.
Help us to use our science for peace and plenty, not for war and
    destruction.
Show us how to use atomic power to bless our children's chil-
    dren, not to blight them.

Save us from the compulsion to follow our adversaries in all
    that we most hate,
Confirming them in their hatred and suspicion of us.

Resolve our inner contradictions, which now grow beyond
    belief and beyond bearing.
They are at once a torment and a blessing: for if you had not
    left us the light of conscience, we would not have to
    endure them.

Teach us to be long-suffering in anguish and insecurity.

Teach us to wait and trust.
Grant light, grant strength and patience, to all who work for
    peace; to our Congress, our President, our military forces,
    and our adversaries.

Grant us prudence in proportion to our power, wisdom in proportion to our science, humaneness in proportion to our wealth and might.

And bless our earnest will to help all races and peoples to travel, in friendship with us,
Along the road to justice, liberty, and lasting peace.

But grant us above all to see that our ways are not necessarily your ways,
That we cannot fully penetrate the mystery of your designs,
And that the very storm of power now raging on this earth reveals your hidden will and your inscrutable decision.

Grant us to see your face in the lightning of this cosmic storm,
O God of holiness, merciful to men.
Grant us to seek peace where it is truly found!

In your will, O God, is our peace! *Amen.*

THOMAS MERTON

JUSTICE AND TRUTH   4

Almighty God, our heavenly Father, guide, we beseech thee, the nations of the world into the way of justice and truth, and establish among them that peace which is the fruit of righteousness; that they may become the kingdom of our Lord and Saviour Jesus Christ.

Book of Common Prayer (USA)

CHILDREN OF ONE FATHER   5

Eternal God, in whose perfect kingdom no sword is drawn but the sword of righteousness, no strength known but the strength of love: So mightily spread abroad thy Spirit, that all peoples may be gathered under the banner of the Prince of Peace, as children of one Father; to whom be dominion and glory, now and for ever.

UNKNOWN

PEACE BUILDERS   6

O God, by whose life-giving grace we become citizens of the household of faith: Grant that the good endeavors of willing people in all nations, fitly framed together, may build an earth-wide family of justice and peace, which finds its home in the kingdom of our Lord and Saviour, Jesus Christ.

Prayers of the Spirit

A WORLD AT ONE WITH ITSELF   °7

O God, who hast appointed a day when the sovereignty of the world shall pass to thee and to thy Christ: Grant that we may now and always choose thy Will as our will, thy Way as our way, thy Peace as our peace; and so lock our fortunes to thy purpose, that we shall be satisfied with nothing less than a world at unity with itself, rejoicing in mutual trust, and enabling all nations to bring their glory and honor into thy kingdom; where thou reignest for ever and ever.

CHARLES HENRY BRENT

THE BOND OF CHARITY   8

Look with thy mercy, O Father of men, upon all thy children in every land, on every sea, and in the thoroughfares of the sky. Hold in thy gracious keeping every burdened heart, encourage every noble hope, strengthen every righteous purpose. Unite in the deathless bond of charity all followers of thy valiant Son, whose Name alone can still the cries of greed and bring to our world the hush of peace. Shatter our fears and our misgivings, and let the light of truth so govern our thoughts and guide our hands, that with all the brotherhood of the sons of God we may acknowledge as our home that kingdom which belongs to our Saviour Jesus Christ.

Prayers of the Spirit

OVER ALL THE WORLD 9

Grant thy people rest, O God, each in his own place and over all the world: deliverance from suspicion, injustice, discord, and despair; relief from want; salvation from evil. And gather them, O Father, by one holy faith, into one family of peace; through Christ our Lord.

UNKNOWN

THE INVINCIBLE SPIRIT 10

O God, our help in ages past, whose mighty hand upheld our fathers through days of perplexity and dread: Come now to us their children in the full power of thine invincible Spirit, and refresh us with a new vision, and the courage to follow wherever it leads; knowing only that it must bring us closer to thee, our hope for years to come; through Jesus Christ our Lord.

J. W. S.

A MORE ABIDING ORDER 11

Behold, O our God, our strivings after a truer and more abiding order. Give us visions which bring back a lost glory to the earth, and dreams which foreshadow that better order which thou has prepared for us. Scatter every excuse of frailty and unworthiness. Consecrate us all with a heavenly mission. Open to us a clearer prospect of our work, and give us strength gladly to welcome and gratefully to fulfill it.

BROOKE FOSS WESTCOTT

A KINGDOM OF HOLINESS   12

O God, who by thy Son Jesus Christ did set up on earth a kingdom of holiness, to measure its strength against all others: Make faith to prevail over fear, and righteousness over force, and truth over the lie, and love and concord over all things; through the same Jesus Christ our Lord.

ERIC MILNER-WHITE *and* G. W. BRIGGS

A SINGLE PEACE   °13

O God, who would fold both heaven and earth in a single vesture of peace: May the design of thy great love redeem the waste of our wraths and sorrows, and give peace to thy Church, peace among nations, peace in our dwellings, and peace in our hearts; through Jesus Christ our Lord.

ERIC MILNER-WHITE

PLACES OF VISION   14

Almighty God, supreme Governor of all men, incline thine ear, we beseech thee, to the prayer of nations; and so overrule the imperfect counsel of men, and set straight the things they cannot govern, that we may walk in paths of obedience to places of vision, and to thoughts that purge and make us wise; through Jesus Christ our Lord.

WOODROW WILSON

A LITANY OF THE BEATITUDES

O God of all goodness and grace, we thank thee for the promises given us through him who came as the Incarnate Word:

Blessed are the poor in spirit, for theirs is the kingdom of heaven;

Blessed are they that mourn, for they shall be comforted;

Blessed are the meek, for they shall inherit the earth;

Blessed are they which do hunger and thirst after righteousness, for they shall be filled;

Blessed are the merciful, for they shall obtain mercy;

Blessed are the pure in heart, for they shall see God;

Blessed are the peacemakers, for they shall be called the children of God;

Blessed are they which are persecuted for righteousness' sake, for theirs is the kingdom of heaven.

We confess the sins and the shortcomings that hold us back from the blessings thou wouldst bestow.

From shallow contentment, and from the pride that makes us rich in our own conceits,

O Lord, deliver us.

From the easy self-pleasing that would shut our ears to the sorrows of the world,

O Lord, deliver us.

From the self-assertion that has no grace of meekness,

O Lord, deliver us.

From lust for the things of earth that may corrupt the love of righteousness,

O Lord, deliver us.

From hardness of heart that holds no compassion for the needy and the distressed,

O Lord, deliver us.

From the divided purpose that gives no full devotion,

O Lord, deliver us.

From irritation and anger that destroy the peace that thou wouldst give,

O Lord, deliver us.

From the softness and self-pity that will not suffer for righteousness' sake,
O Lord, deliver us.

Thou who alone canst save us from the sins that stand between us and thy benediction, grant us, we beseech thee, the blessedness which is offered even to us, the undeserving, who trust the promise of thy Word.

For a teachable and humble spirit, quick to see within us and around us the signs of the kingdom of God,
We beseech thee, O Lord.

For a heart that mourns with those who suffer, and for a conscience that takes upon itself the burden of our human sins,
We beseech thee, O Lord.

For faith that the earth shall be inherited not by the violent and cruel, but by those whom thy gentleness makes great,
We beseech thee, O Lord.

For hunger and thirst after righteousness that shall not cease until thy purpose in us is fulfilled,
We beseech thee, O Lord.

For the spirit of forgiveness and of mercy, as we remember how great is the mercy that we ourselves must ask of thee,
We beseech thee, O Lord.

For sincerity of desire, notwithstanding all our imperfections, and for thy atoning love that may grant us the vision of God which only the pure in heart deserve,
We beseech thee, O Lord.

For patient understanding, and for reconciling grace by which all men may learn to live as thy children in a world at peace,
We beseech thee, O Lord.

For the power that belonged to all thy saints and heroes who dared to be persecuted for righteousness' sake, and for a will in us that can be faithful to the end,
We beseech thee, O Lord.

And the grace of our Lord Jesus Christ, and the love of God, and the fellowship of the Holy Spirit, be with us evermore. *Amen.*

WALTER RUSSELL BOWIE

FOR THE UNITED NATIONS   16

O God, whom the peoples of the world worship under many names, yet who art the Father of all; and who hast put it into the hearts of many nations to work together for mutual security and human progress: Guide, we beseech thee, the members of the Council and Assembly of the United Nations. Press upon them the urgency of their task. Help them to remove the causes of war. In debate, curb every impulse to bitterness, and give faith to build upon every sign of good will and understanding. And grant that this instrument, devised by men, may promote thy will and be used for thy glory, who art the Sovereign of all nations. This we ask through Jesus Christ our Lord.

CHARLES T. WEBB

WORDS AND ATTITUDES   17

O God, who dost rule the destinies of men and nations, we thank thee for every attempt to draw the peoples of the world together in conference. Grant to the representatives of the nations, on whose words and attitudes so much depends, the grace to understand points of view which differ from their own; that each may regard not only his nation's welfare, but thy will for the whole world; through Christ our Lord.

LESLIE D. WEATHERHEAD

HUMILTY AND REVERENCE   18

Almighty God, we pray thee to enlighten all men of science who search out the secrets of thy creation, that their humility before nature may be matched by their reverence of thee. Forbid that we should misuse the fruits of their labors, and grant that the forces they set free may so enrich the life of man that thy Name may be hallowed, both in the search for truth and in the use of power; through Jesus Christ our Lord.

Canadian Draft Prayer Book

POWER IN TRUST   19

Almighty and merciful God, without whom all things hasten to destruction and fall into nothingness: Look, we beseech thee, upon thy family of nations and men, to whom thou hast committed power in trust for their mutual health and well-being. Save us and help us, O Lord, lest we abuse thy gift and turn it to misery and ruin. Draw all men unto thee in thy kingdom of righteousness and truth; uproot our enmities, heal our divisions, cast out our fears, and renew our faith in thine unchanging purpose of peace on earth; for the love of Jesus Christ our Lord.

CYRIL GARBETT

REVELATION   20

O God, who hast revealed thyself in the glory of the heavens and in the burning bush, in the still small voice and in the dread power of nuclear weapons: Make us aware of thy presence as thou comest in judgment through the events of our time. Grant us to stand in awe, and sin not. Enable us to use the fearful powers thou hast permitted us to know, not for man's destruction but for his fulfillment; and lift us above suspicion and fear, that we may bring peace, righteous and just, among all men. This we ask, anxious yet quiet in thee; perplexed, yet certain in thee; weak, yet strong in thee; through the might of him who is the only Saviour of the world, Jesus Christ our Lord.

CHARLES S. MARTIN

LEST WE PERISH   21

Almighty God, whose creative hand we discern in the vastness of the oceans, the strength of the hills, and the unimaginable reaches of space: Grant that as we delve more deeply into the mysteries of the world which thou hast made, we may not forget thy loving purpose for us and for all men, lest we perish in ignorance of the things belonging to our peace; in the Name of Jesus Christ our Lord.

J. W. S.

A NEW STATURE   22

Almighty and eternal God, who hast entrusted the minds of men with the science and skill which can greatly bless or wholly destroy: Grant us a new stature of spirit to match thy trust, that we may use our inventions to thy glory and the benefit of all mankind; through Jesus Christ our Lord.

UNKNOWN

CHRIST, JUDGE OF NATIONS   23

Come among us, O Son of man, in thy glory, and gather the nations before thee. So shall thy righteousness judge our sin, thy strength our weakness, and our wayward thoughts be measured by thy truth. Then in thy power lift us, we pray thee, to that kingdom prepared for us from the foundation of the world, where, with the Father and the Holy Spirit, thou reignest for ever and ever.

Prayers of the Spirit

TO ENRICH LIFE 24

O Thou who dost hold the secrets of nature in thine hand, we praise thee for the gifts of science which have added to man's well-being and deliver him from some of the agonies of pain. We bless thee for the long roll of scientists who rendered self-less service in the exploration of truth, especially those who gave life itself in the battle against disease. We pray thee now to grant illumination to all who seek the cause and cure of diseases that still baffle us, to the end that they too will be conquered. Deliver us from the employment of thy gifts in the destruction of life and reason, whether in war or peace; and hasten the day when science will be used only for the enrichment of life and the advancement of thy kingdom among men; for thy Name's sake, who art the Great Physician and Lover of all mankind.

GODFREY S. PAIN

MISUSED GIFTS 25

O God our Father, from whom all fatherhood in heaven and earth is named: Graciously behold us, thy family. Thou art ever merciful, and makest thy sun to rise on the just and on the unjust; but we have misused thy gifts, marred thy work, and robbed one another of our daily bread. Help us to see and feel our share in the guilt of the world, and grant us thy grace to bring forth fruits worthy of repentance; through Jesus Christ our Lord.

MRS. REINHOLD NIEBUHR

GOD'S BROKEN FAMILY 26

O God, creator of all the ends of the earth and Father of all men, behold thy broken family. Have pity on our tensions, our suspicions, our perplexities. May thy Spirit move mightily upon the hearts and minds of all who guide the stream of history. Surprise us with new wisdom, that we may have clean and sound public policies, and the courage to put them into effect. Heal the earth and sea and sky and the vast spaces that surround them, and let justice come as the dayspring from on high to give light in our darkness, and to guide our feet into the way of peace; through Jesus Christ our Lord.

Prayers of the Spirit

FOR THE HEALING OF THE NATIONS 27

O Lord Jesus Christ, who tookest upon thee to deliver man, and in whom alone is our salvation: Mercifully behold the earth in disquietude, and the peoples in perplexity and fear. Rise, O Sun of Righteousness, with healing in thy wings, and shed upon us deliverance and peace; for the honor of thy holy Name.

WILLIAM FREDERIC FABER

BREAK DOWN THE WALLS 28

O God, who hast made of one all nations to dwell upon the earth, and by thy Son Jesus Christ hast broken down the walls of partition between Jew and Gentile, slave and free, Greek and barbarian: Break down, we beseech thee, all that divides us one from another. Shame our jealousies, lay low our pride, and do away with all race-prejudice; that the bonds of fellowship and mutual service may so unite the East and the West, the North and the South, that we may live in peace together; to the glory of thy great Name.

GILBERT C. BINYON

A KINGDOM TO BE BUILT

Jesus, Lord and brother,
Who at Nazareth didst grow to manhood,
Busy in the sunlit workshop
With eye and hand and brain,
Yet ever dreaming of a kingdom to be built,
World-wide, eternal, not made with hands;
Help us to grow in wisdom,
Loving the things of heaven,
Seeing the world, as with thine eyes,
At its true value;
For the sake of thyself, our Saviour Jesus Christ.

EDWARD D. SEDDING, S.S.J.E.

TO DARE HIGH THINGS

O God, give us a strong sense of the mystery and wonder and beauty of life. Help us to enter by our intuition into the invisible world which surrounds us. May our faith give substance to the things we hope for; may we feel the pressure of thy constant presence which encompasses us. Give wings to our hopes, and rest to our fears. Add to our faith, courage; that, believing in thee and conscious of thee, we may dare high things for thee. Save us from the little faith which makes us the victims of anxieties and fears, and puts us to shame and confusion—we who are the heirs of all the ages and children of the Father Almighty! Give us dignity and worth by sending us some work to do for thee; fire our wills to accomplish something for thy kingdom before we leave this world. May the Spirit that was in Jesus so possess our minds and wills that we may share his indignations, his purpose, and his radiant faith in thee.

WILLIAM SCARLETT

ADVENTURE OF FAITH 31

Heavenly Father, in whom is no darkness at all, nor any shadow cast by turning, forgive our feverish ways—our anxieties, our fears, our uncertainties. We are like children walking willfully and blindly in darkness while the world without is ablaze with light.

Open our eyes that we may see thee, and our minds that we may understand and know thee. Help us to make the great adventure of faith, and discover the secret of peace in finding thee, thou great Companion of our souls.

Then make us persuasive agents among men of thy just and merciful will.

WILLIAM SCARLETT

ADVENTUROUS WILLINGNESS 32

Eternal God, Father of all souls, grant us such a clear vision of the futility of war, that we may the more earnestly strive for peace. Arouse in us, we pray thee, an adventurous willingness to work for international goodwill—to dare bravely, think wisely, act resolutely, and by the power of thy Spirit achieve triumphantly; in the Name of Jesus Christ our Lord.

S. M. E. TROOD

UNDER THE DOMINION OF CHRIST 33

Almighty and eternal Father, who dost will that all things be subject to the dominion of thy beloved Son: We pray thee to heal the nations, wounded and divided by their sins, and knit them together in obedience to the King of kings and Lord of lords, our Saviour Jesus Christ.

Book of Common Prayer
(CHURCH OF INDIA, PAKISTAN, BURMA, AND CEYLON)

RENEWED DEDICATION   34

O God, who hast created man in thine own image; who art
patient with us in our blindness and folly; who dost ever wait
and hope for the obedient response of sons; who didst send
Jesus Christ to teach us a better way of life, though we scorned
him, and though we still refuse to listen to the one Physician
who can heal us: Open our blind eyes; compel us to see what
we are doing; give us new hearts, and wills set upon righteousness and peace. Accept our renewed dedication to follow
Christ's way, and use us, feeble as we are, in the preparation
for thy kingdom—which shines even now, in this hour of judgment, like the heavenly city set upon the far hills. In Christ's
Name.

FREDERICK C. GRANT

ONE EARTHWIDE FAMILY   35

We thank thee, O Father, that progress in science has influ-
enced men to live as one family; that the order, security, and
peace of each country are involved in the order, security, and
peace of all other countries; that the unity of the human family
has always existed in that all its members are equal in their
natural dignity. Open, we beseech thee, the eyes of those who
bear the responsibility of ministering to human need, that
they may see their problem in the context of one earthwide
family under thy Fatherhood; to whom be glory and dominion,
world without end.

FROM PASSAGES IN THE ENCYCLICAL LETTER OF POPE JOHN XXIII
(APRIL 11, 1963)

2

The Higher Patriotism

The time to pray for your enemies is when you have some.

Behold, O God, this our beloved Country:
> The old, the young, the little children; rich and poor, ignorant and learned;
> The laborers and managers of industry; workers in factory and mine, office and home;
> A people of many traditions, many colors, divergent hopes and fears.

Behold America:
> Its mountains and plains, rivers and forests, its inland seas and shining coasts.

Upon this land, upon these people, pour down thy life-giving Spirit of nobility and truth.
> Where there is strife, bring co-operation for the common good;
> Where greed and envy abound, control us with that divine perspective which sees in every man the dignity of a growing soul;
> Where interests clash, set free in us the higher impulse which seeks first thy righteous kingdom, where we may enjoy the glorious liberty of the children of God.

Behold, O Father, this our Nation. Bless it, make it strong with thy strength, and fill it with the beauty of holiness; through Jesus Christ our Lord.

Prayers of the Spirit

FOR OUR COUNTRY °37

Almighty God, who in the former time didst lead our fathers
forth into a wide and bountiful land: Give thy grace, we humbly beseech thee, to us their children, that we may always prove
ourselves a people mindful of thy favor and glad to do thy will.
Bless our nation with honorable industry, sound learning, and
pure manners. Defend our liberties, preserve our unity. Save
us from violence, discord, and confusion, from pride and arrogancy, and from every evil way. Fashion into one happy people
the multitudes brought hither out of many kindreds and
tongues. Endue with the spirit of wisdom those to whom in
thy Name we entrust the authority of government, to the end
that there be peace at home, and that we keep our place among
the nations of the earth. In the time of our prosperity, temper
our self-confidence with thankfulness; and in the day of trouble, suffer not our trust in thee to fail; all which we ask through
Jesus Christ our Lord.

The Book Annexed

TRUE AND ENLIGHTENED   38
LOVE OF COUNTRY

Deepen and purify within us, O Lord, true and enlightened
love of country: a love that rejoices in beauty and ever seeks to
preserve it; a love that could fill our land with happy homes; a
love that will not rest until it has removed the stain of hopeless
poverty and cured the blindness which passes it by. In the
Name of him who wept over his beloved Jerusalem, may we
strive to make our country more worthy of his love, who with
thee and the Holy Spirit ever liveth one God, world without
end.

C. H. S. MATTHEWS

NATIONAL SINS 39

We beseech thee, O God, to forgive those national sins which do so easily beset us: our wanton waste of soil and sea, our desecration of natural beauty, our heedlessness of those who come after us if only we be served; our love of money, our contempt for small things and worship of big things; our complacency, and our pride of life. For these wrongs done to our land and our heritage, as for right things left undone, forgive us, O Lord.

Book of Common Worship
(PRESBYTERIAN CHURCH, USA)

SOUND MOTIVES 40

Make us, O God, lovers of our homes, loyal to our country, and in everything faithful to thee. Keep clean the flame of fire in the inner world of our hearts, that our motives may be sound, our thoughts and deeds honorable. Purify our aspirations, and grant that as they come from thee, so they may return to thee as acceptable deeds, carrying on high our wills made captive to thy service, whose service is perfect freedom; through Christ our Lord.

CHARLES HENRY BRENT

HUMILITY WITH FIRMNESS 41

Almighty God, who hast bidden us to carry in thy Name the sword of the Spirit; who hast made us messengers of peace in a world of strife, and messengers of strife where false peace prevails: Make strong our hand, make clear our voice, give us humility with firmness, and insight with passion; that we may fight not to conquer but to redeem, following the example of thy blessed Son, the Saviour of the world.

GREGORY VLASTOS

WORKING IN HARMONY   42

Grant, O Lord, to those who till the ground, and to those who
employ them, the wisdom to understand thy laws, and the
grace to work in harmony with thy wise ordering of nature.
Enable men of science to discover more secrets of the earth for
the benefit of mankind, and endue our statesmen with unswerving purpose to make just laws. May all work together in the
spirit of fairness and good will, to the end that the fruits of thy
bounty be neither hoarded by the selfish nor squandered by the
foolish, and all may share in the harvest; through Jesus Christ
our Lord.

The Grey Book

NEW INSIGHTS FOR OUR TIME   °43

Almighty and everliving God, who art beyond the grasp of our
highest thought but within the reach of our frailest trust:
Come in the beauty of the morning's light and reveal thyself to
us. Enrich us out of the heritage of seers and scholars and
saints into whose faith and labors we have entered, and quicken
us to new insights for our time; that we may be possessors of
the truth of many yesterdays, partakers of thy thought for
today, and creators with thee of a better tomorrow; through
Jesus Christ, the Lord of the ages.

HENRY SLOANE COFFIN

THE RIGHT USE OF FREEDOM   44

Almighty God, who hast created man in thine own image:
Grant us grace fearlessly to contend against evil, and to make
no peace with oppression; and, that we may reverently use our
freedom, help us to employ it in the maintenance of justice
among men and nations, to the glory of thy holy Name;
through Jesus Christ our Lord.

EDWARD LAMBE PARSONS

JOY AND RESPONSIBILITY 45

O Lord God almighty, who hast made all the nations on the face of the earth to serve thee in the joy and responsibility of freedom: Give us not only a passion for equal justice under law, but also such strength of self-control that we may exercise our liberty with a single desire to promote thy gracious will for all mankind; through Jesus Christ our Lord.

HENRY SCOTT HOLLAND

IN OUR HANDS °46

Almighty Father, remind us ever, we pray thee, that in our hands is all authority but thine; that where there is evil in government, where there is negligence, where there is stupidity, we only, by thy grace, can set it right. Grant us the will to think, to speak, and to meet together in thy Name, since only in understanding one another can we learn thy will for all. So may our laws come ever closer to thine, our governments to the fulfillment of thy kingdom.

MRS. H. H. WALKER LEWIS

THINGS WE OUGHT TO HAVE DONE 47

O God, who through thy Son Jesus Christ hast taught us that true living is not measured by the abundance of possessions, and hast promised to all who seek first thy kingdom of righteousness all things needed for their welfare: Forgive our undue concern for comforts while our brethren lack necessities. Save us from the complacency which makes us shirk our responsibility for people of other lands, or for those in our own land who suffer under disadvantages which we could remove. Let not our blindness or our greed delay the coming of thy kingdom upon the earth, but make plain to us wherein we can now do those things which we ought to have done, and give us the strength to do them; in the Name of Jesus Christ our Lord.

CHARLES T. WEBB

THE TRIUMPH OF OUR AIMS   48

Almighty Father, Maker of the stars, Master of the nations of the earth, we ask thy favor on our country engaged in the audacious and ever-changing, ever-challenging, experiment of democracy. That we may never grow weary of our task because of its difficulties, nor doubt the final triumph of our aims, grant us unconquerable faith, an unswerving belief in men, a confidence that truth if made known will win its way, and infinite patience. Give us flexibility of mind, and a willingness to try new experiments, that we may create the conditions which make men free and equal, enhance human dignity and self-respect, and establish a fair measure of economic security for our people. Bind upon each of us a stern sense of our individual accountability to thee, that we may always devise things which are just, and rising above group or sectional prejudice make the good of all our aim. So shall we take our place among those who labor that government of the people, by the people, for the people, shall not perish from the earth.

WILLIAM SCARLETT

OUR COUNTRY A BLESSING   49

Almighty God, heavenly Father, we pray thee to bless our country, that it may be a blessing to the world. Help us to adopt aims and policies that are in accordance with thy will. May we see ourselves as others see us, and avoid self-deception and hypocrisy. Lead us to sound government, equal justice under law, wise education, and incorruptible media of news. Grant us a true sense of fairness in our dealings with one another, and a spirit of service that will banish pride of place and give equality of opportunity to all. This we ask in the Name of him who taught that only the truth can make men free, thy Son Jesus Christ our Lord.

The Grey Book

WIDEN OUR SENSE OF BROTHERHOOD 50

Almighty God, who dost call us to love thee with heart and soul and mind, and our neighbors as ourselves: Deepen in us, we pray thee, our awareness of thy presence, and widen our sense of brotherhood until all conditions and races of men are known to us and served by us as thy children, even as we are known and loved of thee; through him who is the Redeemer of the world, our Saviour Jesus Christ.

Prayers of the Spirit

SEND OUR MINDS AND HEARTS ABROAD 51

God of our life, who meetest us on every hand in the beauty and bounty of nature, in the love which binds us to the living and the dead, in glimpses of truth, and in the calls of duty: Draw aside the veils and set our spirits face to face with thee. Thine eyes are in every place, for thy thought and love go out to all men. Send our minds and hearts abroad until we too feel our kinship with the world-wide brotherhood of thy children, and crave for all, as for ourselves, health of body, education that frees us from superstition and ignorance, liberty to think and live as sons and daughters of God, a chance to work and a chance to rest, a conscience made sensitive by the ideals of Christ, and a soul that trusts and serves thee in his Spirit; through the same Jesus Christ our Lord.

HENRY SLOANE COFFIN

PEOPLES AND RULERS 52

Almighty God, Ruler of all the peoples of the earth: Forgive, we beseech thee, our short comings as a nation; purify our hearts to see and love truth; give wisdom to our counselors and steadfastness to our people; and bring us at last to that fair city of peace whose foundations are mercy, justice, and good-will, and whose Builder and Maker thou art; through thy Son, Jesus Christ our Lord.

WOODROW WILSON

EACH OTHER'S NEED   53

Almighty God, Maker and Disposer of all things, who hast placed the things necessary for the use of men in divers lands and sundry countries, yea, and unto this end—that all kinds of men should be knit together in unity and love, seeing we all have need one of another's help, one country of another country's commodity, one realm of another realm's gifts and fruits: We beseech thee to preserve and keep all such as travel either by land or by sea, for the getting of things that be necessary for the realms where they dwell, and to give them safe passage both in their going and coming; that having prosperous journeys, they may show themselves thankful to thee and beneficial to their neighbor, and so do business with their merchandise without fraud, guile, or deceit, that the commonweal may prosper and flourish with the abundance of worldly things through their godly and righteous travails; unto the glory of thy Name.

THOMAS BECON

THE SHUTTLE OF COMMERCE   54

Almighty God, the Master Workman of the universe, we thank thee for entrusting to us the task of weaving the threads of human affairs into the fabric of thy purpose for mankind. Give us wisdom in our stewardship as we drive the shuttle of commerce from man to man and nation to nation. May the spirit of responsibility and fair play be our guide in home and club, in factory and office, in rest and recreation. Forbid that we should value things above persons, or surrender honor to the love of gain or the lust for power. Prosper, we pray thee, all efforts to put an end to toil that brings no joy, and wealth that breeds corruption; that the ways of our common life may show forth the majesty and glory of the Maker of all men, world without end.

CHARLES HENRY BRENT

RENEWED IN BEAUTY AND ORDER   55

O God our Father, increase in every nation the sense of human brotherhood, true respect for man and for woman, loyalty in service and charity, happiness in work, and justice in reward; that our homes may be kept safe and pure, our cities renewed in beauty and order, and all the world may reflect the radiance of thy kingdom; through Jesus Christ our Lord.

Book of Common Order
(CHURCH OF SCOTLAND)

THE SUPREME COURT   56

O God of truth and justice, who art a discerner of the thoughts and intents of the heart, and before whose throne all must stand to be judged: Give, we pray thee, to the members of The Supreme Court of the United States, wisdom and understanding to judge aright; that discerning between good and evil, they may help our nation to move in harmony with thy purpose for all mankind; through Jesus Christ our Lord.

Prayers of the Spirit

THE EXECUTIVE   °57

O Lord our Governor, whose glory is in all the world; we commend our nation to thy merciful care, that being guided by thy providence we may dwell secure in thy peace. Grant to the President of the United States, and to all in authority, wisdom and strength to know and to do thy will. Fill them with the love of truth and righteousness, and make them ever mindful of their calling to serve this people in thy fear; through Jesus Christ our Lord.

GEORGE ZABRISKIE

CITY OF PEACE   58

Build, O God, with our hearts and minds and hands, the City of thy peace; and, that our labor be not lost, keep us ever true to him who is the origin and crown of all faith, thy Son Jesus Christ our Lord.

J. W. S.

THE CONGRESS   °59

Most gracious God, we humbly beseech thee, as for the people of these United States in general, so especially for their Senate and Representatives in Congress assembled; that thou wouldest be pleased to direct and prosper all their consultations, to the advancement of thy glory, the good of thy Church, the safety, honor, and welfare of thy people; that all things may be so ordered and settled by their endeavors upon the best and surest foundations, that peace and happiness, truth and justice, religion and piety, may be established among us for all generations. These and all other necessaries for them, for us, and thy whole Church, we humbly beg in the Name and mediation of Jesus Christ, our most blessed Lord and Saviour.

WILLIAM LAUD

FOREIGN POLICY   60

Teach us, O Lord, to see every question of foreign policy in the light of our creed; that we may check in ourselves and in others every temper which makes for war, all ungenerous judgments, all promptings of self-assurance, all presumptuous claims; that being ever ready to recognize the needs and aspirations of other nations, we may, with patience, do whatsoever in us lies to remove suspicions and misunderstandings; and to honor all men in Jesus Christ our Lord.

The Grey Book

NOT THEIR WILL OR OURS, BUT THINE   61

O God, who art kind to us even when we are unthankful or evil, and sendest thy rain whether we are good or bad: May thy Holy Spirit so possess our minds, that acknowledging thee to be the Father of all men, we may from our hearts pray for our enemies—not that their will, but thine, be accomplished through them, even as we pray that thy will and not ours be done in us. This we ask in the Name of him who commanded us to love one another with a love like his own, our Saviour Jesus Christ.

Prayers of the Spirit

OPEN THEIR HEARTS   °62

The everlasting arm of the Lord hold us up, and break all our bonds asunder, and set us upon the Rock in which we may know his presence. So shall the God of Life be with us, teaching us to pray for our enemies that the Lord will open their hearts to see themselves and us; for the honor of his holy Name.

GEORGE FOX

TRUTH AND BEAUTY   63

O God, who by thy Spirit leadest us to seek for truth and to rejoice in beauty: Inspire, we pray thee, the writers, musicians, craftsmen, and all other artists of our day, that in whatever is true and pure and lovely thy Name may be hallowed, and the coming of thy kingdom advanced, for all who have eyes to see and hearts to understand; through Jesus Christ our Lord.

The Grey Book

SPEAKERS AND WRITERS   64

Almighty God, who hast proclaimed thine eternal truth by the voice of prophets and evangelists: Direct and bless, we beseech thee, those who in our generation speak where many listen and write what many read; that they may do their part in making the heart of this people wise, its mind sound, and its will righteous; through Christ our Lord.

The Boys' Prayer Book

FOR TEMPERANCE   65

Almighty God, gracious Father of men, who openest thine hand and fillest all things with plenty: Teach us to use the gifts of thy providence soberly and temperately. Grant, O Lord, that the blessings which thou givest us may minister neither to sin nor to sickness, but to health and holiness and thanksgiving; that in the strength of thy provision we may faithfully and diligently serve thee here, and be counted worthy to be made partakers of thine eternal kingdom; through Jesus Christ our Lord.

Book of Common Order
(CHURCH OF SCOTLAND)

SAFETY ON THE HIGHWAYS   66

Help us, O God, to examine our habits of driving on the roads in the light of thy commandment to love our neighbor as ourself; that thoughtless or selfish acts which endanger life being eliminated, we may offer unto thee a good record of self-discipline and consideration for the safety of all; through Jesus Christ our Lord.

THE EPISCOPAL CHURCHMEN OF MAINE

PROSPERITY WITHOUT CORRUPTION °67

O God, the protector of all who trust in thee, without whom nothing is strong, nothing is holy: Increase and multiply upon us thy mercy; that, thou being our ruler and guide, we may so pass through the good things that are temporal, that we finally lose not those that are eternal. Grant this, O heavenly Father, for the sake of Jesus Christ our Lord.

Book of Common Prayer (USA)

WORTHY OF OUR CHRISTIAN PROFESSION 68

Look, we beseech thee O Lord, upon the people of this land who are called after thy holy Name, and grant that we may ever walk worthy of our Christian profession; that, laying aside our divisions, we may be united in heart and mind to bear the burdens which are laid upon us. Help us to respond to the call of our country according to our several powers; put far from us selfish indifference to the needs of others; and give us grace to fulfill our daily duties with sober diligence. Keep us from all uncharitableness in word or deed, and enable us by patient continuance in well-doing to glorify thy Name; through Jesus Christ our Lord.

Book of Common Prayer
(CHURCH OF IRELAND)

A LITANY FOR EVERY NATION °69

Since God has set before us the great hope that his kingdom will come on earth, and has taught us to pray and work for its coming, let us beseech him to give to the nations of the world a new heart of comradeship, that we may go forward together in the new and living way which Christ has consecrated for us.

O God, the Father of all,
Have mercy upon us.
Creator of heaven and earth,
Hear our prayer.
O Christ, Son of the Father,
Have mercy upon us.
Redeemer of men,
Hear our prayer.
O Spirit of truth,
Have mercy upon us.
Sanctifier of the faithful,
Hear our prayer.

The earth is the Lord's,
And all that therein is.
From waste which leads to famine, from greed which causes hunger, from blindness to the needs of others,
Good Lord, deliver us.
From ruthless exploitation of forest and plain,
Good Lord, deliver us.
From national pride, vainglory, and hypocrisy,
Good Lord, deliver us.
From all that cheapens and degrades man,
Good Lord, deliver us.

The heavens shall declare his righteousness,
For God himself is Judge.
We beseech thee to hear us, O Lord God; and that it may please thee to give to all nations equal justice under law,
We pray thee.

That the leaders of all peoples, wise and incorruptible, fearing only thee, may face one another with candor as fellow-citizens of thy world,

We pray thee.

That each nation may bring its tribute of excellence to the common treasury, without fear and without the lust of domination,

We pray thee.

That thou wilt set straight the things men cannot govern,

We pray thee.

> God shall judge the nations,
>> *And shall rebuke many peoples.*
> They shall beat their swords into ploughshares,
>> *And their spears into pruninghooks.*
> Nation shall not lift up sword against nation,
>> *Neither shall they learn war any more.*
> And none shall make them afraid,
>> *For the mouth of the Lord hath spoken it.*

Hear us, almighty Father; and that we may lay aside the engines of war, and build new instruments of peace,

We pray.

That the scientists of all nations, relieved of the burdens laid upon them by war, may work together in the fight against plague, famine, and every disease that wastes the mind and body of man,

We pray.

Save us, O Lord God, from a servile and slanted press, radio, and screen; and, that thy truth may govern those who speak where many listen and write what many read,

We pray.

Save us from the economic sickness that brings to individuals great poverty or great wealth; and, that thou wilt have mercy upon us all,

We pray.

Give us, O Lord, men and women of incorruptible leadership, who will broaden our horizon and enlarge our vision; and, that our wills may be alert to build a new citadel of justice and fair dealing,

We beseech thee.

O God our Father, have regard to our intercessions, answer them according to thy will, and make us channels of thy redeeming love; through Jesus Christ our Lord.

Amen.

The Lord is great in Zion,
And high above all people.

Not by might, nor by power,
But by my Spirit, saith the Lord of hosts.

They shall come from the east, and from the west, and from the north, and from the south, and shall sit at table in the kingdom of God.

There were great voices in heaven, saying, The kingdoms of this world are become the kingdoms of our Lord, and of his Christ; and he shall reign for ever and ever.

And the voice of a great multitude, as the voice of many waters, was heard saying,

Alleluia: for the Lord God omnipotent reigneth.

Grace be unto us, and peace, from God our Father, and from the Lord Jesus Christ.

Amen.

ARRANGED BY J. W. S.

3

Intercessions

Say not unto thy neighbor, Go, and come again,
and tomorrow I will give; when thou hast it by thee.

PROVERBS 3:28

FOR ALL IN AFFLICTION   70

Most tender and pitiful Father, we beseech thee for those who
are in danger by land or sea or air; for all who are sick or suffering, and for those who draw nigh unto death; for the bereaved
and the sorrowful; for such as have lost the light of reason, or
have fallen into despair; for those passing through worldly
adversity, and any whose hearts are bitter; for such as have
secret trials, and for whom the help of man is vain; and for all
in affliction known to ourselves, whom we name in silence
before thee. . . . Enable all these to look unto thee, O Father;
vouchsafe to them present help, and, if it please thee, a speedy
and merciful deliverance from their distresses; through Jesus
Christ our Lord.

Book of Common Order
(CHURCH OF SCOTLAND)

THE MARKS OF HIS CROSS   71

O Saviour of the world, uplifted that thou mightest draw all men unto thee: We bring thee in tender intercession those who are in pain or sorrow or loneliness, and especially such as are self-imprisoned. May the heart of God unveiled at Calvary be their comfort and their deliverer. And grant that they and we, and all who have looked upon thee in thy passion, may bear the marks of thy Cross upon us, and live in that love which believeth, hopeth, endureth all, and never faileth; for the honor of the holy Name.

HENRY SLOANE COFFIN

1277160

IN DARK VALLEYS   72

O God, who dost never forsake those who trust in thee, nor abandon thy creatures whom thou hast made, but art near to every one of us though we be called to enter dark valleys and go down to the very gates of death; who in all our afflictions art afflicted, and dost save us by thy presence: Be near to all who suffer, especially those crushed and tortured by man's inhumanity to man in war or peace. By thy Spirit lift them up, and enable them to endure as seeing thee who art invisible yet ever near. And bring speedily the day when wars and cruelties shall be no more; through Jesus Christ our Lord.

FREDERICK C. GRANT

THE HEAVY LADEN   73

O God, I would bring before thee the burden of the world's
life:

> All who are far from home and friends.
> All who must lie down hungry or cold.
> All who suffer pain.
> All who are kept awake by anxiety or suspense.
> All who are facing danger.
> All who must toil, or keep watch, while others sleep.

Give to them, I pray, such a sense of thy presence as may turn
their loneliness into comfort, and their trouble into peace. And
to me, O gracious Father, grant the joy of a life surrendered to
Christ's service, and the peace of sin forgiven.

JOHN BAILLIE

THE UNHAPPY   74

O God, the strength of those who walk with thee, without
whom nothing is safe, nothing is tranquil: Confirm, we pray
thee, in all who are unhappy, the knowledge of thy presence;
that, thou being their companion in the way, they may so deal
with their anxieties that at length their hearts may find their
rest in thee; through Jesus Christ our Lord.

J. W. S.

THE DIVINE CHARITY   75

Enlarge our souls, O Lord, with the divine charity, that hoping
all things and enduring all things, we may become agents of thy
healing mercy to the grievances and infirmities of men; through
Jesus Christ our Lord.

A Book of Collects

THE PRACTICE OF BROTHERHOOD 76

Open our eyes, we beseech thee O Father, to the pitiful plight of thine earthwide family, our ears to the unspoken cries of the impoverished and enslaved. Save us from the sin of futile sorrow which only sees and does not act, and stir up our wills to practise that brotherhood which alone befits the kingdom of thy Christ; for his Name's sake, world without end.

Prayers of the Spirit

GIVE A FAIR JOURNEY 77

To our brethren who are travelling or are minded to travel in whatever place, give a fair journey, whether by land or sea, by river, lake, or road. Bring them everywhere to a safe harbor, a quiet harbor. Do thou thyself sail with those that are sailing, and travel with wayfarers in the way. Give them back to their own people in happiness and health. Yea, Lord, and our sojourning also in this life guard through hurt or tempest unto the end.

Liturgy of St. Mark

THE FAINT-HEARTED °78

O God, who hast made all men, and carest for all alike, have pity on those whose strength seems unequal to the battle of life. Encourage and protect them, and give wisdom and patience to those who are trying to help them; for the sake of Jesus Christ our Lord.

ROBERT N. RODENMAYER

THE PROSPEROUS 79

Hear us, O Lord, in behalf of those to whom thou has given the precious gifts of wealth. May they ever praise thee for thy goodness, remembering that all skill and wisdom and strength of body or of mind come from thee, and that they possess nothing which they have not received from thy hand. Teach them that with every gift thou givest responsibility; that thou hast lent them their riches not for their own enjoyment only, but to increase the well-being and happiness of the world. Keep them free from all that wars against simplicity and nobility of life, from pride and vainglory, from love of power, from false ambitions, from contempt of the poor and the unprivileged. Bestow upon them the grace of the Lord Jesus who for our sakes became poor; and may they follow in his footsteps, and spend and be spent in the service of their brothers; for his Name's sake.

SAMUEL MCCOMB

THOSE WHO HAVE FORSAKEN THE FAITH 80

O almighty, merciful, and gracious God and Father, with our whole heart we beseech thee for all who have forsaken the Christian faith, all who have wandered from any portion thereof, or are in doubt or temptation through the corruptors of thy Word; that thou wouldest visit them as a Father, reveal unto them their error, and bring them back from their wanderings; that they, in singleness of heart, taking pleasure alone in the pure truth of thy Word, may be made wise thereby unto everlasting life; through Jesus Christ, thy Son our Lord.

Brandenburg-Nuremberg Order

THE ESTRANGED 81

O Father of lights, who art ever pitiful to the manifold wanderings of the children of men, and hast given us thy holy Word to be a lantern to our feet amid the darkness of this world: Have compassion upon all who, denying the Gospel of thy Son, have become estranged from prayer. Open their hearts to the truth, and help them to become as little children, that they may be wise; through Christ our Saviour.

The Book Annexed

THOSE HARDENED BY SIN °82

Have mercy, heavenly Father, on all who are hardened through the deceitfulness of sin; vouchsafe them grace to come to themselves, the will and the power to return to thee, and the loving welcome of thy forgiveness; through Christ our Lord.

The Book Annexed

FOR THE HANDICAPPED °83

O loving Father, we pray for all who are handicapped in the race of life: the blind, the defective and the delicate, and all who are permanently injured. We pray for those worn with sickness and those who are wasted with misery; and for all unhappy children. May they learn the mystery of the road of suffering which Christ has trodden and the saints have followed, and bring thee this gift that angels cannot bring: a heart that trusts thee even in the dark. This we ask in the Name of him who took our infirmities upon him, the same Jesus Christ our Saviour.

A. S. T. FISHER

FOR THE PARENTS OF A RETARDED CHILD 84

O God of mercy and compassion, behold and bless these people in their need. Fold their child in the arms of thy love; take away all bitterness from their hearts; and give them patience, kindness, and wisdom to choose wisely for their child, who is a whole person in thy sight; in the Name of Jesus Christ our Saviour.

ROBERT N. RODENMAYER

FOR THE BLIND 85

Wonderful art thou, O God, in thy merciful guidance of man. We thank thee for thy revelations whereby men of science have prevented many of thy children from a life of darkness, and have restored sight to many threatened with blindness. We thank thee that thou dost still provide compensations for those who can never see by the light of the sun: the vision of touch, the quickening of other perceptions, a greater skill of mind and hand, and above all a cheery temper. Bless them, and continue them in the sure hope of the great day when they shall see thee face to face; through Jesus Christ our Lord.

UNKNOWN

DEAF-MUTES 86

Almighty Father, whose blessed Son opened the lips of the dumb and the ears of the deaf: Have compassion, we beseech thee, on all who in our time lack powers of speech and hearing, that by faith they may hear plainly the voice of love, and sing thy praises joyfully in their lives; through the same Jesus Christ our Lord.

ERIC MILNER-WHITE

LEPERS   °87

Almighty and merciful Father, whose Son Jesus Christ went
where he was most needed and showed his love for all: Make
us alert to the needs of the ten million people throughout
the world who are afflicted with leprosy. Imprint upon our
minds the knowledge that much of their suffering is no longer
necessary, that they need not be shut off from the rest of us,
and can live normal and useful lives. Stir up our wills, we pray
thee, so to act on this knowledge that these our brothers may
be set free from an enslavement and ignominy forced upon
them by callousness or fear. Make us generous in providing for
their relief, and bless those who are spending their lives in the
service of these men and women and children who are precious
in thy sight. We ask thee in the Name of him whom thou hast
appointed to heal the broken-hearted and set at liberty those
that are bruised, our Saviour Jesus Christ.

                                                         J. W. S.

FOR VICTIMS OF A DISASTER   88

Almighty Father, who hast set our lives on a planet where both
beauty and danger are to be found, graciously hear our prayer
for those who have been overtaken by the disastrous . . . (famine, flood, earthquake, fire, plague) . . . in . . .

    Comfort the maimed and suffering; fortify with a sense of
thy presence all who are overcome by fear and distress. Watch
with those who anxiously watch. Draw thou near to the dying
and bless them with thy peace. Sustain and uphold the
bereaved.

    Endue with tenderness and strength the doctors and
nurses, and all who help them minister to human need. And
grant that we, our hearts moved by compassion like thine own,
may share the burdens of these our brothers and so fulfil the
law of Christ, thy Son our Lord.

                                            Prayers of the Spirit

THE LONG WATCHES OF THE NIGHT 89

Come, O Lord, with healing in thy wings, and shield with thy sustaining presence all who wait for comfort in the long watches of the night. Speak thy word of assurance to every troubled heart; uphold the spirits of those who miss their loved ones; and help us all to know that thou art ever faithful, keeping watch above thine own; through Jesus Christ our Lord.

J. W. S.

SHARING THE BURDENS 90

Blessed Lord Jesus, who for our sakes bore sorrow and want and death: Grant that we may follow thee in courage and self-denial. Help us to minister to the afflicted, bring relief to the destitute, and share the burdens of the heavy laden; and in all who are poor or desolate give us grace to discern the image of thyself, for the honor of thy holy Name.

The Grey Book

A LITANY FOR ALL WORKERS °91

O God, who hast made us a royal priesthood, that we might offer unto thee prayer and intercession for all sorts and conditions of men, hear us as we pray.

For all who toil in the burden and the heat of day, that they may enjoy the rewards of their industry, that they may not be defrauded of their due, and that we may never cease to be mindful of our debt to them, remembering with gratitude the multitude of services which must be performed to make our life tolerable:

We pray thy grace and pledge our concern, O God.

For those who have authority and power over their fellow men, that they may not use it for selfish advantage, but be guided to do justice and to love mercy:

We pray thy grace and pledge our concern, O God.

For those who have been worsted in the battles of life, whether by the inhumanity of their fellows, their own limitations, or the fickleness of fortune, that they may contend against injustice without bitterness, overcome their own weakness with diligence, and learn how to accept with patience what cannot be altered:

We pray thy grace and pledge our concern, O God.

For the rulers of the nations, that they may act wisely and without pride, may seek to promote peace among the peoples and establish justice in our common life:

We pray thy grace and pledge our concern, O God.

For teachers and ministers of the word, for artists and interpreters of our spiritual life, that they may rightly divide the word of truth, and not be tempted by pride or greed or any ignoble passion to corrupt the truth to which they are committed:

We pray thy grace and pledge our concern, O God.

For prophets and seers and saints, who awaken us from our sloth, that they may continue to hold their torches high in a world darkened by prejudice and sin, and ever be obedient to the heavenly vision:

We pray thy grace and pledge our concern, O God.

O Lord, who hast bound us together in this bundle of life, give us grace to understand how our lives depend upon the courage, the industry, the honesty and integrity of our fellow men; that we may be mindful of their needs, grateful for their faithfulness, and faithful in our responsibilities to them; through Jesus Christ our Lord.

REINHOLD NIEBUHR

A PRAYER OF INTERCESSION 92

Almighty God, our heavenly Father, who lovest all and forgettest none, we bring to thee our supplications for all thy creatures and all thy children.

For all whom we love and for whom we watch and care:

We beseech thee to hear us.

For all who have blessed us with kindness, led us with patience, restored us with their sympathy and help, and whose charity has covered a multitude of our sins:

We beseech thee.

For all who have wished or done us ill, that thou wouldst turn their hearts to penitence and ours to blessing:

We beseech thee.

For all dumb creatures; that men may be merciful, and touched with a feeling of their infirmities:

We beseech thee to hear us.

For all prisoners and captives, and all suffering from oppression, that thou wilt manifest thy mercy towards them, and make the heart of man merciful as thine own:

We beseech thee.

For all on whom thou hast laid the cross of suffering, the sick in body and the feeble in mind; for all who are in danger, necessity, and tribulation; and all who travel by land or by water:

We beseech thee.

For all who have been bereaved of relatives and friends, or are troubled by the suffering or sin of those they love:

We beseech thee to hear us.

For all who are visited by worldly loss, that in the dark and cloudy day they may find the peace of God:

We beseech thee to hear us.

For all who are absorbed in their own grief, that they may be raised to share the sorrows of their brethren, and know the secret and blessed fellowship of the Cross:

We beseech thee.

For all who do justly, love mercy, and walk humbly with God, that grace and peace may rest upon them:

We beseech thee.

For all who are suffering because of their faithfulness to conviction and duty, that renunciation may bring strength, and sacrifice, joy; and that they may have thy grace, who seest in secret, and come at last to an open reward:

We beseech thee to hear us, O God.

For all perplexed by the deeper questions of life, over-shadowed with doubt, and concerned lest even in thought they should depart from thee, that light may arise in their darkness:

We beseech thee to hear us.

For the careless, the scornful, the lovers of darkness rather than light, that they may be delivered from the bonds of iniquity:

We beseech thee.

For all who are tried by passionate temptations, or cold ambitions, or mean suggestions, that thy mercy may be their salvation:

We beseech thee to hear us, O God.

For all who are lonely and sad in the midst of others' joys, that they may know God as their Friend and Comforter:

We beseech thee.

For the infirm and aged, and all who are growing weary with the journey of life; and for all who are passing through the valley of death; that they may find comfort and strength in God, and light at evening time:

We beseech thee to hear us.

For all forgotten by us, but dear to thee:

We beseech thee to hear us, O God.

O God our Father, have regard to our intercessions, answer them according to thy will, and make us the channels of thine infinite pity and helpfulness.

JOHN HUNTER

ALL WHO NEED OUR PRAYERS   93

Finally, O Lord, we commend to thy goodness those dear to us, whom we name in our hearts; those forgotten by us but dear to thee; and all who desire or need our prayers. By thy mercy guard them, in thy presence keep them, now and forever.

Prayers of the Spirit

4

The Church

THE PEACE OF CHRIST   94

O Lord Jesus Christ, who saidst unto thine Apostles, Peace I
leave with you, my peace I give unto you: Regard not our sins,
but the faith of thy Church; and grant us that peace and unity
which is according to thy will; who livest and reignest with the
Father and the Holy Ghost, one God, world without end.

Book of Common Prayer (USA)

THE CHURCH OF CHRIST   95

O God of unchangeable power and eternal light, look favorably
on thy whole Church, that wonderful and sacred mystery; and
by the tranquil operation of thy perpetual providence carry out
the work of man's salvation, and let the whole world feel and
see that things which were cast down are being raised up, and
things which had grown old are being made new, and all things
are returning to perfection through him from whom they took
their origin, even Jesus Christ our Lord.

WILLIAM BRIGHT

CHRIST IN THE MIDST   °96

Grant, O God, that thy Church may not glory in numbers or
wealth or learning or power, but only in this: that Christ is in
her midst, who is Wealth and Wisdom and Might, and with
whom two or three are as a multitude; through the same Jesus
Christ our Lord.

JOHN U. STEPHENS

BEST OF ALL PILOTS   97

O God, who as the best of all pilots dost guide the ship of thy
Church while it is tossed to and fro amid the perils of this
world: Grant that we, who by thy Spirit are so marvellously
launched forth upon the unfathomable dangers of this stormy
sea, may be guided by the rudder of thy right hand into the
port of heaven; through Jesus Christ our Lord.

Mozarabic Missal

THE CHURCH IN A CHANGING ORDER   98

O God, we pray for thy Church, set today amid the perplexities
of a changing order, and face to face with new tasks. Fill us
afresh with thy Spirit, that we may bear witness boldly to the
coming of thy kingdom; and hasten the time when the knowledge of thyself shall fill the earth as the waters cover the sea;
through Jesus Christ our Lord.

UNKNOWN

DISCRETION AND BOLDNESS 99

We beseech thee, O Lord, to guide thy Church with thy perpetual governance, that it may walk warily in times of quiet, and boldly in times of trouble; through Christ our Lord.

AFTER ST. FRANCIS

WITH VALIANT FAITH °100

Almighty and everlasting God, who of thy great goodness hast given us an enduring fellowship of faith: Strengthen us, we pray thee, by the mighty indwelling of thy Holy Spirit, that we may show forth our gratitude in steadfast discipleship. Bless all who have prospered the life of our [Diocese], and grant that encouraged by their good examples we may continue to serve thee with valiant faith; through Jesus Christ our Lord.

CHARLES FRANCIS HALL

GREGORY THE GREAT °101

Almighty and merciful God, who didst raise up in Gregory the Great a servant of the servants of God, by whose labor the people of England were brought into the knowledge of the Catholic and Apostolic faith: Preserve in thy Church evermore a thankful remembrance of his devotion, that thy people, being zealous in every good work, may receive with him and thy servants everywhere the crown of glory that fadeth not away; through Jesus Christ our Lord.

Prayer Book Studies XVI

LITANY OF THE CHURCH   102

O God the Father, from whom the whole family in heaven and
    earth is named;
O God the Son, given to be head over the Church;
O God the Holy Spirit, the bond of peace;
O Holy Trinity, eternal love,
    Have mercy upon us.

By the ministry of healing and forgiveness; by thy seeking and
saving the lost, by thy words of eternal life,
    Help us, good Lord.
By thy calling and training of the twelve apostles; by thy promise to build thy Church; by thy institution of the holy sacraments,
    Help us, good Lord.

By the love shown in thy crucifixion; by the power of thy resurrection; by the glory of thy ascension; and by the indwelling of
thy Holy Spirit,
    Help us, good Lord.
That it may please thee to strengthen and enlarge thy holy
Church in every land, and to unite all those who profess and
call themselves Christians,
    We beseech thee, good Lord.
That thy Church may strive not for its own safety, but for the
world's salvation,
    We beseech thee, good Lord.
That thy Church may proclaim the gospel throughout the
whole earth,
    We beseech thee, good Lord.
That thou wilt grant to all ministers of thy word and sacra-
ments the spirit of wisdom, power, and love,
    We beseech thee, good Lord.
That thou wilt give to all thy people grace to understand and
believe thy word, and to show forth their faith in their lives,
    We beseech thee, good Lord.

That thou wilt remove from us all hatred, prejudice, and narrowness of thought, so that we may rejoice in all that thou revealest,

We beseech thee, good Lord.

That thou wilt so guide us in all perplexities of belief and conduct, that we may hold fast that which is true, and faithfully confess thee before men,

We beseech thee, good Lord.

That regardless of the praise or contempt of the world, thy Church may worship thee in spirit and in truth,

We beseech thee, good Lord.

And as we pray for the Church universal, so let us pray for God's blessing on the Church in this place.

Here may the faithful find salvation, and the careless be awakened.

Amen.

Here may the tempted find help, and the sorrowful comfort.

Amen.

Here may the weary find rest, and the strong be renewed.

Amen.

Here may the aged find peace, and the young be inspired.

Amen.

Now unto him that is able to do exceeding abundantly above all that we ask or think,

According to the power that worketh in us,

Unto him be glory in the Church and in Christ Jesus unto all generations for ever and ever.

Amen.

The Grey Book

O most holy Spirit of God, from whom alone the fulness of wisdom and life proceed: Come in thine everlasting power and glory upon the Church and into the hearts of men, and bring to the world a new birth of holiness, new understanding of truth, and new unity in a love like that which shone forth in the life of our Lord and Saviour, Jesus Christ.

ERIC MILNER-WHITE

THE GOOD NEWS OF OUR DAY   °104

O God, our Shepherd, give to the Church a new vision and a new charity, new wisdom and fresh understanding, the revival of her brightness and the renewal of her unity; that the eternal message of thy Son, unhampered by man-made traditions, may be hailed as the good news of our day; through him who maketh all things new, the same Jesus Christ our Lord.

The Grey Book

PURGE AND STRENGTHEN THE CHURCH   °105

Gracious Father, I humbly beseech thee for thy Holy Catholic Church. Fill it with all truth, in all truth, with all peace. Where it is corrupt, purge it. Where it is in error, direct it. Where it is superstitious, rectify it. Where anything is amiss, reform it. Where it is right, strengthen and confirm it. Where it is in want, furnish it. Where it is divided and rent asunder, make up the breaches of it, O thou Holy One of Israel.

WILLIAM LAUD

PETER THE ROCK °106

O Christ, the Son of the living God, who calledst Simon Peter to be the rock whereon thy Church should be built: Grant that thy household, mindful of its apostolic lineage, may so hear what the Spirit saith unto the churches, that it may in every age bring forth out of its treasure things new and old; to thy honor and glory, who with the Father and the same Spirit livest and reignest ever, one God, world without end.

FRANCIS C. LIGHTBOURN

THANKSGIVING FOR THE REFORMATION 107

O almighty and eternal God, who hast chosen out of the world in all times and places those who have believed in thee: We give thee thanks for thy holy people who served thee under the patriarchs and prophets; we praise thy holy Name for those who in their generation have believed in thine only-begotten Son, his incarnation, passion, and glorious resurrection. To thee we give most high worship for his saving Gospel, for thy wonderful grace in him, and for that holy foundation which is his body, the Church. Especially do we praise thee for thy servants, our fathers in Christ, through whom thou didst restore and recall thy Church to its first profession in the faith of the Gospel. Blessed art thou, O Lord, and greatly to be praised, and highly exalted for ever.

Mercifully defend thy Church, O Lord God, from all enemies of thy saving Word. Bless the work of the Gospel in all lands. Strengthen and renew thy Church; enable it effectively to make known to the world the truth of the Gospel; make it, in our time, the bearer of the blessings of light and love and peace to the world, that all men may see and know that thou art God.

And as thou hast enriched the life of man through the Reformation of the Church, we beseech thee to preserve its fruits to the blessing of our generation and generations to come. Preserve thy Word, all good education, our liberties and civil privileges; and maintain ordered government and fair dealing among nations and men. Enrich our manhood and womanhood with high ideals and honorable purposes. Inspire us to maintain the heritage of the faith and liberty, which we have received from our forefathers.

And to thee, Father, Son, and Holy Ghost, one God, be all glory and praise, now and evermore.

GEORGE R. SELTZER

A UNITY OF LOVE 108

O God the Father, good beyond all that is good, fair beyond all that is fair, in whom is calmness, peace, and concord; do thou make up the dissensions which divide us from each other, and bring us back into a unity of love which may bear some likeness to thy divine nature. And as thou art above all things, make us one by the unanimity of a good mind; that through the embrace of charity and the bonds of affection, we may be spiritually one, as well in ourselves as in each other; through that peace of thine which maketh all things peaceful, and through the grace, mercy, and tenderness of thy Son, Jesus Christ.

ST. DIONYSIUS

FOR ALL MANKIND   109

Accept, O Lord, our intercessions for all mankind. Let the light
of thy Gospel shine upon all nations; and may as many as have
received it live as becomes it. Be gracious unto thy Church,
and grant that every member of the same, in his vocation and
ministry, may serve thee faithfully. Send down thy blessings,
temporal and spiritual, upon all our relations, friends, and
neighbors. Reward all who have done us good, and pardon all
those who have done or wish us evil. Be merciful to all who are
in any trouble, and do thou, the God of pity, administer to
them according to their several needs; for his sake who went
about doing good, thy Son our Saviour Jesus Christ.

Book of Common Prayer (usa)

ONE IN LOYALTY   110

Almighty God, in whom are calmness and concord, we pray
thee to heal the divisions of thy Church which separate brethren from one another. While there are diversities of knowledge,
and we cannot all be of the same mind, make us one in loyalty
to thy Son Jesus Christ, and in the endeavor to enthrone him
Lord of lords. Deliver us from blindness, prejudice, intoler-
ance, and evil-speaking, that by the charity of our temper and
thought we may show forth the beauty and power of the faith
we profess, and thus commend it to the world; through Jesus
Christ our Lord.

HENRY SLOANE COFFIN

THE MIND OF CHRIST 111

O God, who didst make the Gospel for a united Church, let not our misunderstanding of its message obstruct thy saving work. Show us wherein we are sectarian or contentious in spirit, and give us grace to confess our faults, that we may become more worthy to bind up the Church's wounds. Help us to place the truth above our conception of it, and joyfully to recognize the presence of thy Holy Spirit wherever he may choose to dwell among men; and so endue us with the mind of Christ, that in him we may all become one.

CHARLES HENRY BRENT

UNITY OF FAITH 112

Almighty God, grant to us who now are terrified on every side, that we may learn to raise our eyes above the world and to hope for that which is now hidden from us: even that in executing thy judgments on the Church as well as on unbelievers, thou wilt be merciful to the whole world, so that we may be gathered into the unity of faith. And may we labor to devote ourselves wholly to thy service and cultivate brotherly concord among ourselves, until we shall at length enjoy that eternal inheritance which has been obtained for us by the blood of thine only-begotten Son, our Saviour Jesus Christ.

JOHN CALVIN

NO WALL OF DIVISION 113

Lord Jesus Christ, who art the Door by whom if any man enter he shall be saved: Open unto us who knock, that evermore abiding within the ample household of thy redeeming charity, we may live as true brothers of all whom thou dost love; for thy Name's sake.

J. W. S.

THE TRUE BREAD 114

Almighty God, who gave us the true Bread from heaven, even thy Son Jesus Christ: Grant that our souls may be so fed by him who gives health unto the world, that abiding in him and he in us, we may be filled with the power of his deathless life; through the same Jesus Christ our Lord.

The Grey Book

A SHORT LITANY 115

From arrogance and impatience; from willful misunderstandings of each other's problems,
> *Deliver us, good Lord.*

From envy and strife, and whatever else hinders us from union and concord,
> *Set free our hearts and minds.*

From failure to recognize the work of the Holy Spirit wherever He may please to dwell,
> *Good Lord, deliver us.*

From the stupidity which refuses to rejoice in truths which thou has revealed to those who are separated from us, and from unwillingness to learn from them,
> *Deliver us, O Lord.*

AN ANGLICAN BISHOP

REACHING FORTH OUR HANDS 116

Lord Jesus Christ, who didst stretch out thine arms of love on the hard wood of the Cross, that all men might come within the reach of thy saving embrace: So clothe us in thy Spirit, that reaching forth our hands in loving labor for others we may bring those who know thee not to the knowledge and love of thee; for the honor of thy holy Name.

CHARLES HENRY BRENT

OUR UNIVERSAL NEED 117

O God, who hast blessed us with the knowledge of the gospel of Christ, make us glad to give of ourselves and of our possessions to carry his gospel to peoples and nations who lack what we have had. Not unto us, O Lord, but unto thee be the glory and the praise for the light which has been kindled in our own land. Cleanse us from all false pride of race and blood, from self-complacency, and from indifference to the hunger of any human soul. Teach us that life can nowhere find fulfilment except in Christ, and that in our universal need of him we are one with all mankind. And this we ask in the name of him who died for the whole world, and who only in a world redeemed can manifest his risen life.

WALTER RUSSELL BOWIE

ENLARGE THE BORDERS 118

Deliver thy Church, O Lord, from all evil, perfect it in thy love, strengthen it by thy Word and Sacraments; and so enlarge its borders, we pray thee, that thy Gospel may reach all nations, and the faithful be gathered from all the ends of the earth into the kingdom which thou has prepared for those who love thee; through Christ our Lord.

SWEDISH LUTHERAN CHURCH

ALL CHRISTIANS 119

O Thou whose eye is over all the children of men, and who hast called them, by the Prince of Peace, into a kingdom not of this world; send forth his Spirit speedily into the dark places of our guilt and woe, and arm it with the piercing power of thy grace. May it reach the heart of every oppression, and make arrogancy dumb before thee. Let it still the noise of our strife and the tumult of the people; put to shame the false idols of every mind; carry faith to the doubting, hope to the fearful, strength to the weak, light to the mourner; and more and more increase the pure in heart who see their God. Commit thy word, O Lord, to the lips of faithful men, or to the free winds of thine invisible providence, that soon the knowledge of thee may cover the earth, as the waters cover the channels of the deep. And so may thy kingdom come through Christ, thy Son our Lord.

JOHN HUNTER

ALL NATIONS AND ALL FLOCKS 120

O God, we pray for thy Church which exists from end to end of the world. Bless all the nations and all the flocks; the peace of heaven give into all their hearts, and also the peace of this life graciously bestow upon us. The kings, the armies, the rulers, the councils, the multitudes; our neighbors, our comings in and our goings out, adorn with all peace, O King of peace. Give unto us thy peace, for thou hast given us all things. Possess us, O Lord, for we know none other beside thee. Thy holy Name we utter. May our souls live through thy Holy Spirit, and let not the death of sin prevail against us thy servants nor against all thy people.

Coptic Offices

THE CHURCH THE BODY OF CHRIST   121

Quicken our wills, O God, by the touch of thy life-giving
Spirit; that awakening to the inward light of thy presence, we
may think those thoughts and do those deeds which alone can
make us worthy to be called the Body of thy Son, our Saviour
Jesus Christ.

Prayers of the Spirit

GRACE TO LOSE OURSELVES   122

O God, help us to understand the condition and the place in
which we find ourselves, and to see clearly the possibilities, the
great dangers, the glorious opportunities, that confront thy
Church today. Give us the grace to lose ourselves, with all our
hopes and plans, in thy wise and good purposes, and to think
only of the advancement of thy kingdom. By the power of thy
Spirit lift us above ourselves, and use us as thou wilt; so that in
the end our lives may really count and our efforts succeed; but
only as we are one with thee—through Christ who is our Life.

FREDERICK C. GRANT

EVERY SUNDAY   °123

O God, who makest us glad every Sunday with the remembrance of the glorious resurrection of thy Son our Lord: Grant
us such blessing through our worship of thee, that we may
spend the remainder of the week in thy service; through the
same Jesus Christ our Lord.

Book of Common Prayer (USA)

RELIGIOUS EDUCATION 124

Almighty God, our heavenly Father, who hast committed to thy holy Church the care and nurture of thy children: Enlighten with thy wisdom those who teach and those who learn, that rejoicing in the knowledge of thy truth, they may worship thee and serve thee from generation to generation; through Jesus Christ our Lord.

Book of Common Prayer (USA)

THIS GATHERING OF PEOPLE °125

Be pleased, heavenly Father, to come in thy Holy Spirit to this gathering of thy people, and grant that as we look up to thee in penitence and praise, thou wilt look down on us in pardon and in grace; through Jesus Christ our Lord.

SAMUEL M. SHOEMAKER

THE MORE EXCELLENT WAY 126

Almighty and everlasting God, from whom come wisdom and understanding: Be present, we humbly beseech thee, with thy servants about to deliberate upon things that make for the maintenance, well-being, and extension of thy holy Church; and grant that, seeking only thy honor and glory, we may be guided in all our consultations to perceive the more excellent way, and may have grace and strength to follow the same; through Jesus Christ our Lord.

Book of Common Prayer
(THE EPISCOPAL CHURCH IN SCOTLAND)

AT A QUIET DAY OR RETREAT   °127

O Lord Jesus Christ, who didst say to thine Apostles, Come ye apart into a desert place and rest awhile, for there were many coming and going: Grant, we beseech thee, to thy servants here gathered, that they may rest awhile at this present time with thee. May they so seek thee, whom their souls desire to love, that they may both find thee and be found of thee. And grant such love and such wisdom to accompany the words which shall be spoken in thy Name, that they may not fall to the ground, but may be helpful in leading us onward through the toils of our pilgrimage to the rest which remaineth to the people of God; where, nevertheless, they rest not day and night from thy perfect service, who with the Father and the Holy Ghost livest and reignest ever one God, world without end.

R. M. BENSON

FOR RELIGIOUS COMMUNITIES   128

Almighty God, whose Son, our Master and our Lord, humbled himself to be the Servant of all: We pray thee to sanctify and bless the Religious Communities which thou has called to labor in this [Province]. Grant to them such increase in numbers as is according to thy will. May their members ever advance in charity and holiness, in humility and wisdom; so that abiding in thee, and proving what are the riches of thy grace, they may be a blessing in the midst of thy holy Church; who livest and reignest God, world without end.

Book of Common Prayer
(CHURCH OF INDIA, PAKISTAN, BURMA, AND CEYLON)

THANKSGIVING FOR THE CHURCH °129

O God, most glorious, most bountiful, accept, we humbly beseech thee, our praises and thanksgivings for thy holy Catholic Church, the mother of all who bear the Name of Christ. We bless thee for the faith which it hath conveyed in safety to our time, the mercies by which it hath enlarged and comforted the souls of men, the virtues which it hath established upon earth, and the holy lives by which it glorifieth both the world and thee; to whom, O blessed Trinity, be ascribed all honor, might, majesty, and dominion, now and for ever.

LANCELOT ANDREWES

THE BLESSINGS OF THE CHURCH 130

Almighty God, whose mercy is over all thy works: We praise thee for the blessings which have been brought to mankind by thy holy Church throughout all the world. We bless thee for the grace of thy Sacraments; for our fellowship in Christ with thee, and with one another; for the teaching of the Scriptures, and for the preaching of thy Word. We thank thee for the holy example of thy saints in all ages; for thy servants departed this life in thy faith and fear, and for the memory and example of all that has been true and good in their lives; humbly beseeching thee that we may be numbered with them in the great company of the redeemed in heaven; through Jesus Christ our Lord.

Book of Common Prayer
(CHURCH OF IRELAND)

5

Ministers of Christ

GOD'S WORKMAN °131

Lord God, who hast placed me in thy Church as a pastor, thou seest how unfit I am to fulfil this great and responsible office. Were it not for thy counsel I would long ago utterly have failed. Therefore do I call upon thee for guidance. Gladly will I give my heart and voice to thy service. I want to teach, and I long to be taught continually through thy Word. Use me as thy workman, O Lord. Only do not thou forsake me; for if I were alone, I would bring everything to naught.

MARTIN LUTHER

FAITHFUL STEWARDS 132

Raise up among us, O Lord, prophets and teachers; and when the Holy Spirit shall command us to separate any to the work whereto thou dost call them, grant that we may hear and obey, so that the senders and the sent alike may do thy will, and bide thy time, and see thy glory; through Jesus Christ our Lord.

Book of Common Worship
(CHURCH OF SOUTH INDIA)

FISHERS OF MEN °133

O Master of thy disciples, who, at the sea of Galilee, didst cast thy net for souls, bringing four fishermen into the captivity which set them free, and sending them forth to fetch men to the eternal shore for life and not for death: We ask to have our part in this great work. Give us the eye to see the soul which hides itself; then give us the word that wins it. In every man may we behold God's Son, and call him forth, till all the waves of this troubled world shall have no power to hold him back from thee. So, when this age is past, and again thou standest by the sea at the morning watch and callest us, we may all live in thine everlasting light.

CORNELIUS B. SMITH

JOHN CHRYSOSTOM 134

O God, who didst give grace to thy servant John eloquently to declare thy righteousness in the great congregation, and fearlessly to bear reproach for the honor of thy Name: Mercifully grant unto all bishops and pastors such excellency in preaching, and fidelity in ministering thy Word, that thy people may be partakers with them of the glory that shall be revealed; through Jesus Christ our Lord.

Prayer Book Studies XVI

A FIRE OF ZEAL °135

Almighty God, whose Son Jesus Christ came to cast fire upon the earth: Grant that by our prayers and witness a fire of zeal may be kindled which will pass from heart to heart, and cause the light of thy truth to shine forth bright and clear; through the same Jesus Christ our Lord.

UNKNOWN

SPEAKING THE TRUTH IN LOVE   136

Grant we beseech thee, merciful Lord, to all who contend for
the Faith, the grace never to injure it by clamor or impatience,
but so to present thy precious truth that men will see in it thy
goodness and thy beauty; for the honor of thy holy Name.

AFTER WILLIAM BRIGHT

A PRAYER OF PREACHERS   137

O Holy Spirit, who hast called us to be prophets, and who
showest to them that love thee the things that were and the
things that are and the things that shall be hereafter: Before
we dare to speak of thee to others, reveal thyself to us. Breathe
into our hearts the mysteries which no man can learn except by
prayer. Take every faculty which thou hast given, and make it
servant to every trust which thou dost reveal. Give us thy message, save us from our own; then help us to utter, without fear
and without favor, each word of thine. Give us grace so to
preach that we may build, not destroy; guide, not bewilder.
And add, O God, thy gift of sympathy, without which no man
can be thy prophet. Give us power with souls. Help us to forget ourselves in remembering thee. O Spirit of holiness, in-
flame our hearts and inspire our lips, for the sake of Jesus
Christ our Lord.

CORNELIUS B. SMITH

LOVE AND POWER AND SKILL   °138

Almighty God, whose blessed Son called his disciples and sent
them forth to be his witnesses among the people: Grant us
such a measure of his love and power and skill, that through
us many may be drawn to him in the fellowship of his Church,
and find the abundant life which he promised to those who
love thee; through the same Jesus Christ our Lord.

SAMUEL M. SHOEMAKER

FIRES OF FAITH AND COURAGE 139

Almighty God, we pray for those whom thou hast called to minister in spiritual things. Grant them so to proclaim thy Word that the careless may be awakened, the sorrowing comforted, the tempted made strong, and the heavy-laden refreshed. When heart and flesh fail, be thou their strength. Keep alive within them the fires of faith and courage, that they may never despair of the world or of themselves. May they be willing to bear the reproach of Christ, and even to be counted fools for his sake, if only they may win some souls to truth and goodness. Consecrate them to a divine simplicity of purpose, that they may renounce all earthly prizes and ambitions and answer, with glad hearts, thy call to work with thee for the redemption of the world; through him whom thou has made Lord of thy kingdom, our Saviour Jesus Christ.

SAMUEL MCCOMB

A PRAYER OF PRIESTS 140

O God, who hast called us to be thy priests, to live in heaven yet on earth, to talk with thee and with men: Make us, we beseech thee, deeply sensible of the sacredness of our work. Turn our thoughts from titles and robes to love and sacrifice. Save us from the poison of self-conceit, in which all priesthood dies. Give to us the vision of thyself which thou didst give to Peter, James, and John, upon the mount, and to Saul upon the plain. When we stand at thine altar, when we walk in the highway, when we counsel men in darkness, when we go among the sick, the dying, and the dead, grant us always so plainly to see thy heaven that we may show it upon earth. We ask of thee this priesthood, O God, through Christ our Saviour, to whom be honor and worship for evermore.

CORNELIUS B. SMITH

6

Scholars

THE DESIRE TO LEARN °141

O God, who alone canst uphold the minds of men: Endue us, we pray thee, with a desire to learn which shall worthily answer to thy desire to teach. Give us a clear knowledge of ourselves, and a true understanding of our fellow men; and so lead us out of the darkness of ignorance and doubt into the light of thy truth, as it is revealed to us in thy Son, our Saviour Jesus Christ.

HENRY SYLVESTER NASH

ALERT AND HOPEFUL °142

O God, who hast preserved thy Church through the fall of empires, the decay of cultures, and the perplexity of reformations: We beseech thee for thy world in which a new Age is coming to birth. Keep our spirits alert and hopeful. Help us so to understand ourselves and our times that we may pass through critical study to sure conviction. Raise up in our midst scholars who shall be prophets and apostles. Despite the voices of those who would hold us back, preserve us from either impatience or cynicism; that thy kingdom may be known on earth, thy saving health among all nations; through Jesus Christ our Lord.

ROBERT N. RODENMAYER
and SHERMAN E. JOHNSON

COURAGE AND HUMILITY   143

O God, who has founded thy Church to be the pillar and support of the truth: Grant that all who claim membership therein may really love and follow truth. Save us from slipshod or dishonest thinking. Forbid that we should turn away from any question either because we do not know, or because we fear to give, the answer. May we never regard as enemies those who reach conclusions which differ from our own. Strengthen us to read and think and work with courage and humility, confident that if we seek the truth we shall not lack the guidance of thy Spirit; through Jesus Christ our Lord.

A New Prayer Book

FOR THEOLOGICAL STUDENTS   °144

O Lord Jesus Christ, who dost command thy disciples to proclaim the glad tidings of thy saving love to all mankind: Pour out thy Holy Spirit, we beseech thee, on all who are in training for service in thy Church. Give them the seeing eye, the hearing ear, and the ready will to receive and preach thy glorious truth. Bless them with the spirit of discipline and concentration, and enable them to worship, to work, and to witness wherever they may be sent. Hear us, O loving Saviour, whom with the Father and the Holy Spirit we worship, ever one God, world without end.

Canadian Draft Prayer Book

THOMAS AQUINAS   145

Almighty God, who hast enriched thy Church with the singular learning and holiness of thy servant Thomas: Grant us to hold fast the true doctrine of thy Son our Saviour Jesus Christ, and to fashion our lives according to the same; to the glory of thy Name and the benefit of thy holy Church; through Jesus Christ our Lord.

Prayer Book Studies XVI

THE TWO-FOLD RAY OF GRACE °146

Creator, God ineffable, who from the treasures of thy wisdom hast formed nine orders of angels, and hast placed them in a wonderful way above the empyrean: most fittingly hast thou arranged the parts of the universe. Thou, I say, who art called the true fountain of light and wisdom, and the supreme origin; deign to shed upon the darkness of my intellect the two-fold ray of thy grace in which I was born: remove the perversity and darkness, the inexperience and ignorance of my heart. Thou who makest the tongues of infants eloquent, instruct mine, and pour upon my lips the grace of thy benediction. Grant me keenness of intellect, the power of retention, subtlety in interpretation, ability to learn, copious grace of speech. Order my footsteps, direct my progress, finish my course, thou, who with the Father and the Holy Spirit livest and reignest, O God, worthy of praise, full of glory, blessed for ever and ever.

ST. THOMAS AQUINAS

THE KEY OF KNOWLEDGE °147

O God of manifold wisdom, who didst send thine only Son to be a teacher of mankind; let the spirit of thy truth dwell among the scholars of thy Church, and make them ever mindful that without thee they can bear no fruit. Grant them diligence to labor for thy glory with the gifts which thou has given them. Give them strength and patience to seek the key of knowledge, that they may endeavor with prudence and understanding to distinguish the good from the evil, the wisdom of God from the wisdom of the world. So in the end may they by their works show forth the treasures of knowledge, for the advancement of thy kingdom on earth. This we ask in the Name of him who taught the way of God in truth.

GLANVILLE DOWNEY

7

The Bible

When thy word goeth forth, it giveth light and understanding unto the simple.

PSALM 119:130

WRITTEN FOR OUR LEARNING   148

Blessed Lord God, who hast caused the holy Scriptures to be written for our learning: Grant us so to hear them, read, mark, learn, and ponder them, that relying with patience on the power of thy holy Word, we may embrace, and ever hold fast, the blessed hope of everlasting life which thou hast given us in thy Son, our Saviour Jesus Christ.

Book of Common Prayer (USA)

THE IMPERISHABLE MESSAGE   149

O God, who didst inspire Mark the Evangelist to set forth in his Gospel those mighty acts whereby thou hast wrought our redemption: Grant that thy Word, in its wingèd might, may so possess thy people, that by them thy Son Jesus Christ may send out from East to West the sacred and imperishable message of eternal salvation; through the same Christ our Lord.

FRANCIS C. LIGHTBOURN

HOLDING FAST TO THE WORD °150

O God, who didst inspire Luke the Physician to set forth the glorious deeds of our Saviour Jesus Christ, and the signs and wonders wrought by his Apostles: Grant that we, being led by thy Spirit and holding fast to the word of the Gospel, may go from strength to strength till we attain to the excellency of the knowledge of Christ Jesus our Lord, to whom be glory for ever and ever.

FRANCIS C. LIGHTBOURN

NOT ONLY HEARERS °151

O God, who hast caused to echo in us thy divine and saving words, illuminate our souls, sinners though we are, for the understanding of those things which have been read and taught to us before this time; that we may be seen to be not only hearers of thy spiritual hymns, but doers of good works, and so achieve an undisguised faith, a life without reproach, and a blameless citizenship in Christ our Lord; with whom thou art blessed, along with thy most holy and good and life-giving Spirit, now and forever and for the ages of ages.

Liturgy of St. James

A GOOD HOPE 152

O God, by whose command the order of all time runs its course: Forgive, we pray thee, the impatience of our unbelief, and make perfect that which is lacking in our faith; and while we tarry thy fulfilment of the ancient promises, grant us to have a good hope because of thy Word; through Jesus Christ our Lord.

WILLIAM REED HUNTINGTON

OUR HEARTS AFIRE °153

Grant, O God, that whensoever our eyes are holden that we see thee not, our hearts may be attentive to thy holy Word, and burn within us as it is opened to us by thy Son, our Saviour Jesus Christ.

The Book Annexed

THE MYSTERY OF THE GOSPEL 154

Help us, we pray thee O God, so to honor the truths which we have learned from thee, that our lives may unveil the mystery of the Gospel proclaimed by thy Son, our Saviour Jesus Christ.

J. W. S.

COMMENDING THE GOSPEL 155

Renew in us, O Lord, the desire to understand thy Gospel, and commend it by word and by deed; that thy way may be known on earth, thy saving health among all people; through Jesus Christ our Lord.

J. W. S.

8

Holy Communion

At Holy Communion we are invited to the Lord's Table with the condition that we repent of our sins; that we are in love and charity with our neighbors, and intend to live a new life. Then we are bidden to draw near in faith that God will see us when we are a long way off, in faith that with him we shall eat and drink and be merry, knowing that we have been lost but are found.

GEORGE W. BARRETT

HE WAS THE WORD 156

> He was the Word, that spake it:
> He took the bread and brake it;
> And what that Word did make it,
> I do believe and take it.

UNKNOWN

DRAW NEAR 157

This is the day which the Lord hath made; we will rejoice and be glad in it.

This is the feast which the Lord hath spread; we will draw near and partake of it.

This is the Body and Blood of Christ; let us go forth in his Name.

FRANCIS C. LIGHTBOURN

THE SACRAMENT OF LOVE   158

Incline thy merciful ear, O Lord, to our prayers, and enlighten
our hearts by the grace of thy Holy Spirit, that we may worthily approach these sacred mysteries and love thee with an everlasting love through Jesus Christ our Lord.

The Grey Book

MAKE THYSELF KNOWN TO US   159

Cleanse us, O God, from our secret faults and mercifully
absolve us from our presumptuous sins, that our Lord Jesus
Christ when he cometh may find in us a mansion prepared for
himself.

As watchmen look for the morning, so do we look for thee,
O Christ; come with the dawning of the day and make thyself
known to us in the breaking of bread, for thou art our God for
ever and ever.

We praise thee, we bless thee, we worship thee, we glorify
thee, O Father, Son, and Holy Ghost, ever one God, world
without end.

A. S. T. FISHER

MIGHTY ACTS IN OUR MIDST   160

O God, whose word is nigh unto us, and whose mighty acts
are wrought in our midst: Grant us so to hear the Gospel of
thy Son Jesus Christ, and to celebrate the memorial of his Passion and Resurrection, that we thy people, being many, may be
one body in him in whom thou dost reconcile the world unto
thyself, the same Christ our Lord; to whom be glory for ever
and ever.

FRANCIS C. LIGHTBOURN

THE EYES OF OUR UNDERSTANDING

O God, Creator of light, Originator of life, Author of grace, Founder of the ages, Bestower of knowledge, Treasure of wisdom, Teacher of holiness, Receiver of pure prayers, Benefactor of our souls; who givest to the faint-hearted who put their trust in thee, to behold those things which the angels desire to gaze upon; who hast led us back from the depths of darkness to light, who givest us life from death, who hast brought us by thy grace from slavery to freedom, who hast destroyed the darkness of sin in us through the coming of thine only-begotten Son: Do thou now, our Lord and Master, through the visitation of thy most holy Spirit, enlighten the eyes of our understanding, that we may partake without fear of this eternal and heavenly food, and sanctify us fully, in soul, body, and spirit, that we may pray to thee with thine holy disciples and apostles; . . . and deem us worthy, O Lord and Master, lover of mankind, with boldness and without accusation, in a clean heart and with unashamed face and with consecrated lips, to call upon thee.

Liturgy of St. Mark

THIS BREAD, THIS WINE   162

In this bread, O God, we see the sign of hunger both of body and of soul, a hunger to be satisfied with nothing less than thee. In the brokenness of the bread we hold the mystery of this world and of our flesh, wherein all things are under the judgment of death, yet by their poverty and shame share in the glory of communion where faith, hope, and love make all things new. In this wine we are bought by the precious blood of him who died upon the Cross that we might enter into a new covenant, by which we are bound in freedom to the everlasting God, to be thy children for ever and ever.

SAMUEL H. MILLER

HIS SUSTAINING PRESENCE 163

O God, of whose gift come sunshine, and friendship, and the glory of a summer's day, who in the common things of daily life givest to us thy very self, making of bread and wine the sacrament of thy sustaining presence: Strengthen and refresh us, that we may seek thee eagerly, find thee surely, and serve thee faithfully; through Jesus Christ our Lord.

LETTICE SHANN

ACCOMPLISHED AND CONCLUDED 164

Accomplished and concluded, O Christ our God, so far as in us lies, is the Mystery which thou hast ordained. For we have had the memorial of thy death, we have seen the figure of thy resurrection, we have been filled with thine unending life. We have enjoyed thine inexhaustible delight, of which vouchsafe to count us all worthy also in the world to come; through the grace of thine eternal Father, and thy holy, and good, and quickening Spirit, now and ever, world without end.

Liturgy of St. Basil

OUR SOULS ARE FED 165

O Lord God almighty, we thank thee with all our hearts that thou hast fed our souls with the body and blood of thy most dear Son. And we beseech thee unfeignedly so to illuminate our minds with thy Holy Spirit, that we may daily increase in strength of faith to thee, in assuredness of hope in thy promises, and fervency of love toward thee and our neighbor; to the glory and praise of thy holy Name.

MILES COVERDALE

SPIRITUAL FOOD 166

Almighty and everliving God, we heartily thank thee for that thou dost feed us, who have received these holy mysteries, with the spiritual food of the most precious Body and Blood of our Saviour Jesus Christ, assuring us thereby of thy favor and goodness towards us, and that we are members incorporate in his mystical body, the blessed company of all faithful people, and heirs, through hope, of thy everlasting kingdom. And we beseech thee, heavenly Father, so to assist us with thy grace, that we may continue in that holy fellowship, and do all such good works as thou hast prepared for us; through the same Jesus Christ our Lord, to whom, with thee and the Holy Ghost, be all honor and glory, world without end.

THOMAS CRANMER

IN TRUE COMMUNION 167

Preserve, O Lord, in true communion, those who were guests at thy table, and let the splendor of this day shine upon the work and labor of the week.

The Church in Germany in Prayer

NEWNESS OF LIFE 168

Strengthen, O Lord, the hands which have been held out to receive thy holy things, that they may ever serve thee. Grant that the tongues which have uttered the Holy, holy, holy, may speak the truth; that the eyes which have seen thy great love may also behold thy blessed hope; that the feet which have trod thy house may walk in the region of light; and that we who have received the living Body and Blood of Jesus Christ may be re-stored with newness of life, through the same Jesus Christ our Lord.

Liturgy of Malabar

MAKE US WORTHY 169

Remember, O Lord, what thou hast wrought in us, and not what we deserve; and as thou hast called us to thy service, make us worthy of our calling, through Jesus Christ our Lord.

Leonine Sacramentary

THE HOLY FLAME 170

O God, who hast ordained the sacrament of the altar: Grant that with honorable and faithful lives we may guard the holy flame of thy presence which thou hast given us in these sacred mysteries; through Jesus Christ our Lord.

Prayers of the Spirit

HIS STRONG HAND IN BLESSING 171

O God, the great and wonderful One, look down upon us thy servants who have bowed our heads to thee. Stretch out thy hand, strong and full of blessings, and bless thy people. Guard thine inheritance that we may ever and in all things glorify thee, the only living and true God; the holy and consubstantial Trinity, Father, Son, and Holy Spirit, now and forever and for the ages of ages.

Liturgy of St. James

SILENT THANKFULNESS °172

And now, O Father, that we have told thee of our inmost needs, and have received thy precious Gift, we linger a moment to worship thee in silent thankfulness.

AFTER WILLIAM BRIGHT

9

Encounter with God

*Thou shalt show me the path of life; in thy presence is the
fulness of joy, and at thy right hand there is pleasure
for evermore.*

PSALM 16: 12

THE SWIFT AND SOLEMN TRUST   °173

Eternal God, who committest to us the swift and solemn trust
of life; since we know not what a day may bring forth, but only
that the hour for serving thee is always present, may we wake
to the instant claims of thy holy will; not waiting for to-mor-
row, but yielding to-day. Lay to rest, by the persuasion of thy
Spirit, the resistance of our passion, indolence, or fear. Consecrate with thy presence the way our feet may go, and the hum-
blest work will shine, and the roughest places be made plain.
Lift us above unrighteous anger and mistrust into faith and
hope and charity, by a simple and steadfast reliance on thy sure
will; and so may we be modest in our time of wealth, patient
under disappointment, ready for danger, serene in death. In
all things draw us to the mind of Christ, that thy lost image
may be traced again, and thou mayst own us as at one with him
and thee.

JAMES MARTINEAU

WITH AUSTERE MERCY   174

O Lord, thy steps are slow
And thy patience is greater than our heart.
With austere mercy thou drawest us to thee.
Day by day thou preparest us
To receive thee aright.
Thou constrainest us to leave aside the hope
Of following foolish wishes;
Thou makest us wait for thy counsel.
Thou teachest us to pray for thy perfect gift,
To ask for that which alone is needful.
Thou, Lord, art holy;
In thee alone is truth
And the peace of truth.
Let us hear thy voice.
Bless us in the knowledge of thy will.
Thy will alone makes us free.

The Church in Germany in Prayer

A PURE INTENT   °175

Almighty God, who alone gavest us the breath of life, and alone canst keep alive in us the breathing of holy desires; we beseech thee for thy compassion's sake to sanctify all our thoughts and endeavors, that we may neither begin any action without a pure intent nor continue it without thy blessing; and grant that, having the eyes of our understanding purged to behold things invisible and unseen, we may in heart be inspired with thy wisdom, in work be upheld by thy strength, and in the end be accepted of thee as thy faithful servants, having done all things to thy glory, and thereby to our endless peace.

ROWLAND WILLIAMS

JOY OR PAIN   °176

O Lord, by all thy dealings with us, whether of joy or pain, of light or darkness, let us be brought to thee. May we value no treatment of us simply because it makes us happy or because it makes us sad, because it gives or denies what we want, but may all that thou sendest us draw us to thee; that knowing thy loving wisdom, we may be sure in every disappointment that thou art still caring for us, in every darkness that thou art enlightening us, and in every enforced idleness that thou art still using us: yea, in every death giving us life, as in his death thou didst give life to thy Son, our Saviour Jesus Christ.

PHILLIPS BROOKS

AT HIS HAND   °177

We would receive all at thy hand. If it should be honor and glory, we would receive them at thy hand; if it should be ridicule and insults, we would receive them at thy hand. Oh let us be able to receive either the one or the other with equal joy and gratitude; there is little difference between them, and for us there would be no difference if we thought only of the one decisive thing: that it comes from thee.

SØREN KIERKEGAARD

GOD'S CONTINUAL HELP   178

Direct us O Lord, in all our doings, with thy most gracious favor, and further us with thy continual help; that in all our works begun, continued, and ended in thee, we may glorify thy holy Name, and finally by thy mercy obtain everlasting life; through Jesus Christ our Lord.

Book of Common Prayer (USA)

THE GLADNESS OF HIS PRESENCE   179

Eternal God, who in thy redeemed and holy ones of old hast
manifested thy wonderful love and power: Grant that we, finding thee whom they have found, and loving thee whom they
have loved, may come to dwell with them and thee for ever, in
the gladness of thy glorious presence; through Jesus Christ our
Lord.

Book of Common Order
(CHURCH OF SCOTLAND)

THE THOUGHTS OF OUR HEARTS   180

Almighty God, unto whom all hearts are open, all desires
known, and from whom no secrets are hid: Cleanse the
thoughts of our hearts by the inspiration of thy Holy Spirit,
that we may perfectly love thee, and worthily magnify thy holy
Name; through Christ our Lord.

Book of Common Prayer (USA)

A GREATER LOVE   181

O God, the God of all goodness and grace, who art worthy of a
greater love than we can either give or understand: Fill our
hearts with such love toward thee that nothing may seem too
hard for us to do or suffer in obedience to thy will; and grant
that thus we may become daily more like unto thee, and finally
obtain the crown of life which thou hast promised to those
who unfeignedly love thee; through Jesus Christ our Lord.

The Grey Book

THE LIGHT OF GOD'S LOVE   182

Most loving Father, who willest us to dread nothing but the
loss of thee, and to cast all our care on thee who carest for us:
Preserve us from faithless fears and worldly anxieties, and grant
that no clouds of this mortal life may hide from us the light of
that Love which is immortal, and which thou hast manifested
unto us in thy Son, our Saviour Jesus Christ.

WILLIAM BRIGHT

BEYOND OUR DREAMS   183

O God, who hast prepared for those who love thee such good
things as pass man's understanding: Pour into our hearts such
love toward thee, that we, loving thee above all things, may
obtain thy promises, which exceed all that we can desire;
through Jesus Christ our Lord.

Book of Common Prayer (USA)

FROM DAY TO DAY   °184

Grant, O our God, that we may know thee, love thee, and
rejoice in thee; and if in this life we cannot do these things
fully, grant that we may at least progress in them from day to
day; for Christ's sake.

ST. ANSELM

AT HOME WITH GOD   185

O God, whether a man be on land or at sea or in the air, he
hath need of thee; whether he be at home or far abroad, among
friends or strangers or enemies, thy comradeship shall steady
him; whether he be sick or well, in despair or gladness, perplexed or at ease, thought of thee shall strengthen him;
whether he know thee or not, thou shalt not forsake him; thy
mercy shall be greater than his waywardness, thy faith in him
stronger than his doubt of thee. Whether his heart be broken
or his spirit proud, thy mercy will guide him with patience
until he enters the eternal kingdom, where all men are as children before thee. Whether he has too much or too little of this
world's goods for his own good; whether his reputation is better than his soul, or his soul better than his reputation; whether
he knows much of this world's wisdom or little, thou shalt walk
with him until at last his eyes waken from their blindness and
he shall see thy Light; then he will be thy son indeed, and
wherever he may be, he shall be at home with thee.

SAMUEL H. MILLER

THE SIMPLICITY OF A GREAT PURPOSE   186

O Spirit of grace, who withholdest thy blessing from none:
Take from us the tediousness and anxiety of a selfish mind, the
unfruitfulness of cold affections, and the weakness of an incon-
stant will; that with the simplicity of a great purpose and the
power of a well-ordered soul, we may pass through the toils
and watches of our pilgrimage grateful for all that renders the
burden of duty light, and even in strong trouble rejoicing to be
deemed worthy of the severer service of thy will; through Jesus
Christ our Lord.

JAMES MARTINEAU

Eternal Spirit, thou dwellest in light unapproachable, beyond the power of our thought to comprehend or our imagination to portray. Yet thou art revealed to us in the order of the world we live in, in the truth our minds discover, in the inward presence of thy Spirit, and above all in Christ, thy Son. With reverent hearts we worship thee.

We would bring our fragmentary lives into the presence of thy wholeness. We would bring our transient thoughts into the light of thine eternity. We would bring our restless spirits into the calm strength of thine everlasting purpose.

See what complaints we have brought into thy sanctuary against the circumstances that have fretted us, against the human friends who have failed us, against the enemies who have wronged us, and even against the justice of thine order that has hurt us. Teach us, nevertheless, we beseech thee, to search our own lives, to see that each man is his own destiny, that each soul is its own heaven and its own hell. Send us back into our own souls to find there by thy grace, peace and power, and adequacy to conquer life. May we be victors and not victims.

O God, we would escape from ourselves this hour, from our little and partial selves, from our mean and selfish selves. We would escape from our fragmentary and broken selves into thy greatness. Teach us once again the everlasting mystery that only as we lose ourselves in something higher than ourselves can we find ourselves.

To this end give us a great faith to live by. From doubt and disillusionment, from cynicism and rebellion, deliver us, good Lord. For uncertainty give us confidence. Though we may not see all things clearly, let us see some great things plainly that we may live by them. O God, give us light enough to walk by.

Give us wisdom to live by, we beseech thee. We who walk so often blindly through the tortuous labyrinth of life, give us a clue this day. Let us have vision to see the way we ought to take through some perplexing circumstance. Let high decisions be made on the right side of great questions in thy sanctuary.

Give us love to live by, we pray thee. Enlarge our sympathies; deepen our understandings and compassions. Save us from resentfulness. Cast down within us pettiness and meanness, and lift us up to largeness of mind and heart that we may have the grace to take within the compass of our care those whom by prejudice we have shut out or through dislike have hurt.

Give us great causes to live for. O God, we thank thee for this difficult and serious time, this generation of many dangers and many open doors. Save us from living on a small scale in a great age. Open the eyes of some youths here to causes worth giving life to, that they may be glorified, not alone by what they are, but by what they identify themselves with. Lift us up into better days in the nation. Build justice into our economic order. Grant vision and courage to our statesmen. Make us equal to our international responsibilities and opportunities. And grant that we all may play a part in the things that matter most in our time, so that we may leave this world a fairer home for thy family.

We ask it in the Spirit of the Master.

HARRY EMERSON FOSDICK

TRUE JOYS 188

O Almighty God, who alone canst order the unruly wills and affections of sinful men: Grant unto us thy people that we may love the thing which thou commandest, and desire that which thou dost promise; that so, among the sundry and manifold changes of the world, our hearts may surely there be fixed where true joys are to be found; through Jesus Christ our Lord.

Book of Common Prayer (USA)

COME AMONG US   °189

Raise up, we pray thee O Lord, thy power, and come among us
with thy great might; that whereas through our sins we are hin-
dered in running the race that is set before us, thy bountiful
grace and mercy may speedily help and delivery us; through
Jesus Christ our Lord.

Book of Common Prayer (USA)

CHANGES AND CHANCES OF LIFE   190

Assist us mercifully, O Lord, in these our supplications and
prayers, and dispose the way of thy servants towards the attain-
ment of everlasting salvation; that among all the changes and
chances of this mortal life, we may ever be defended by thy
most gracious and ready help; through Jesus Christ our Lord.

Book of Common Prayer (USA)

OUR ADVERSARY   191

We confess before thee, O God, that those things are to be
condemned in ourselves which have led us astray from Christ,
from thee, and from unity in the Light. Help us to see that
they must also be executed and killed—stoned with the Living
Stone, and run through with the Living Sword, and hammered
down with the Living Hammer to pieces, and burnt up with
the Living Fire, and so made an end of. For that which leads
into Looseness, Whimsies, Imaginations, False Visions, though
it be condemned, yet if it be not executed, is in danger to rise
again; and if it rise again, and get over us, it will be our Ruler.
Him therefore let us resist, steadfast in the faith of our Saviour
Christ.

GEORGE FOX

THROUGH NARROW LANES

Help me, O Captain of my salvation, to fight my way through the narrow lanes of self-discipline and up the steeps of virtue, till by thy grace I reach the pure air of freedom in the fortress of thy love.

CHARLES HENRY BRENT

GOD EVER FAITHFUL

O God, who art, and wast, and art to come, before whose face the generations rise and pass away; age after age the living seek thee, and find that of thy faithfulness there is no end. Our fathers in their pilgrimage walked by thy guidance, and rested on thy compassion: still to their children be thou the cloud by day, the fire by night. Where but in thee have we a covert from the storm or shadow from the heat? In our manifold temptations, thou alone knowest and art ever nigh: in sorrow, thy pity revives the fainting soul: in our prosperity and ease, it is thy Spirit only that can wean us from our pride. O thou sole source of peace and righteousness! take now the veil from every heart, and join us in one communion with thy prophets and saints who have trusted in thee and were not ashamed. Not of our worthiness, but of thy tender mercy, hear our prayer.

JAMES MARTINEAU

ARMOR OF LIGHT

Almighty God, give us grace to cast off the works of darkness and put on the armor of light, now in the time of this mortal life, in which thy Son Jesus Christ came to visit us in great humility; that when he shall come in glorious majesty to judge both the quick and the dead, we may rise to the life immortal; through him who liveth and reigneth with thee and the Holy Ghost, now and ever.

Book of Common Prayer (USA)

CLOTHED WITH CHRIST 195

O God our Father, give to the nations of the world a new heart of comradeship, the old man of ignorance and cruelty being done away, and the new man put on, renewed in knowledge, to serve the brethren; that every people may bring its tribute of excellence to the common treasury without fear and without the lust for dominance, and the world may go forward in the new and living way consecrated for us by him who with thee and the Spirit of truth ever liveth one God, Our Saviour Jesus Christ.

The Grey Book

WORK AS A HIGH CALLING °196

Almighty God, our heavenly Father, who declarest thy glory and showest forth thy handiwork in the heavens and in the earth: Deliver us, we beseech thee, in our several callings, from bondage to the service of self; that we may do the work which thou has given us to do in truth, in beauty, and in righteousness, with singleness of heart as thy servants, and to the benefit of our fellow men; for the sake of him who came among us as one that serveth, thy Son Jesus Christ our Lord.

Book of Common Prayer (USA)

THE SUN TOO BRIGHT °197

Grant unto us, almighty God, in every time of sore distress, the blessing of the forgiveness of our sins. In time of darkness give us hope; in sickness of body give us quiet courage; and when life is a burden and pleasure a weariness, the sun too bright and friends too mirthful, restore us by thy Spirit of calm, and smile upon us with thy quietude.

Services for Broadcasting

THE ROYALTY OF INWARD HAPPINESS   198

Grant me, O Lord, the royalty of inward happiness, and the serenity which comes from living close to thee. Daily renew in me the sense of joy, and let thine eternal Spirit dwell in my soul and fill every corner of my heart with light and grace; that bearing about with me the infection of a good courage, I may be a diffuser of life, and meet all ills with thankfulness to thee for thy great mercies; to whom be praise and glory forever.

L. H. M. SOULSBY

THE SOVEREIGNTY OF GOD   199

Almighty God, whose sovereign purpose none can make void: Give us faith to stand calm and undismayed amid the tumults of our day, knowing that thy kingdom must come and thy will be done, to the eternal glory of thy Name.

ERIC MILNER-WHITE *and* G. W. BRIGGS

JOYFUL OBEDIENCE   200

Help us, O Father, to know thy will, and knowing it, to devote ourselves to the advancement of thy kingdom with that joy which accompanies the doing of thy will in heaven; where thou reignest, God for ever and ever.

Prayers of the Spirit

THE STRENGTH I NEED   201

O Thou, through whom alone I can have true life: Take hold upon me and within me, with thy might mightily, and give me the strength I need.

WINFRED RHOADES

THE SHAPE OF OUR LIVES 202

Draw our affections, O Lord, up to the heights where thou dwellest, that, our hearts being set not on things seen but on things unseen, we may be filled with the vision of thy beauty, and our lives shaped according to thy pattern; through Christ our Lord.

CHARLES HENRY BRENT

TO FULFILL GOD'S INTENT 203

Our Father, who in Holy Writ hast been likened unto a potter working at his wheel, taking the unformed clay and molding it into a likeness pleasing to him; who if a flaw is revealed in the vessel, or a distortion, or weakness, doth not cast it aside as useless or of no account, but doth put it again on the wheel, patiently shaping it toward Beauty: So take and use us, thy faltering children. Bring us again under the discipline of thy love and thy justice: confirm and fulfill in us thine intent: mold us into the likeness of the men and women thou didst mean us to be. And grant us continual growth in knowledge and love of thee, and in courageous dedication to thy will; through him who still could be the Saviour of our world.

WILLIAM SCARLETT

TO STEP FORWARD WITH FAITH 204

O Lord, when I am bewildered and the world is all noise and confusion around me and I don't know which way to go and am frightened, then be thou with me. Put thy hand on my shoulder and let thy strength invade my weakness and thy light burn the mist from my mind. Help me to step forward with faith in the way I should go.

AVERY BROOKE

WALKING IN HIS SIGHT 205

O heavenly Father, in whom we live and move and have our being: So guide and govern us by thy Spirit, that amid all the cares and occupations of our daily life we may not forget thee, but ever remember that we are walking in thy sight; through Christ our Lord.

Book of Common Prayer
(ANGLICAN CHURCH OF CANADA)

FAMILIARLY KNOWN TO US 206

Almighty God, since by our dullness we are so fixed to earth that when thou stretchest forth thine hand to us we cannot always reach thee: Grant that by thy Spirit we may so lift our affections to thee that thou become familiarly known to us, until at length we arrive at the fruition of the full and perfect glory laid up for us in heaven; where with thy Son and the Holy Ghost thou livest, one God for ever and ever.

JOHN CALVIN

10

True Christian Graces

What I am I am and say not. Being is the great explainer.

H. D. THOREAU

O Thou in whose boundless being are laid up all treasures of wisdom and truth and holiness, grant that through constant fellowship with thee the true graces of Christian character may more and more take shape within my soul:

The grace of a thankful and uncomplaining heart:

The grace to await thy leisure patiently and to answer thy call promptly:

The grace of courage, whether in suffering or in danger:

The grace to endure hardness as a good soldier of Jesus Christ:

The grace of boldness in standing for what is right:

The grace of preparedness, lest I enter into temptation:

The grace of bodily discipline:

The grace of strict truthfulness:

The grace to treat others as I would have others treat me:

The grace of charity, that I may refrain from hasty judgment:

The grace of silence, that I may refrain from hasty speech:

The grace of forgiveness towards all who have wronged me:

The grace of tenderness towards all who are weaker than myself:

The grace of steadfastness in continuing to desire that thou wilt do as now I pray.

JOHN BAILLIE

UNCLAIMATIVE LOVE 208

O Thou who dost love my soul, make me, I pray, a worthy lover of souls. Fill me with an unwearied, unclaimative love, keen of perception, strong of fibre, that can help others to be their best selves, even as thy Son set free in others powers they did not know they had; through the same Jesus Christ our Lord.

L. H. M. SOULSBY

COURAGE, GAIETY, QUIET MIND 209

Lord, behold our family here assembled. We thank thee for this place in which we dwell; for the love that unites us; for the peace accorded us this day; for the hope with which we expect the morrow; for the health, the work, the food, and the bright skies, that make our lives delightful; for our friends in all parts of the earth, and our friendly helpers in this place. Let peace abound in our small company. Purge out of every heart the lurking grudge. Give us grace and strength to forbear and to persevere. Offenders, give us the grace to accept and to forgive offenders. Forgetful ourselves, help us to bear cheerfully the forgetfulness of others. Give us courage and gaiety and the quiet mind. Spare to us our friends, soften to us our enemies. Bless us, if it may be, in all our innocent endeavors. If it may not, give us the strength to encounter that which is to come, that we be brave in peril, constant in tribulation, temperate in wrath, and in all changes of fortune, and down to the gates of death, loyal and loving one to another. As the clay to the potter, as the windmill to the wind, as children of their sire, we beseech of thee this help and mercy for Christ's sake.

ROBERT LOUIS STEVENSON

A PRAYER OF HUSBAND AND WIFE   210

O God, who out of all the world hast let us find one another
and learn together the meaning of love, let us never fail to hold
love precious. Let the flame of it never waver or grow dim, but
burn in our hearts as an unwavering devotion and shine through
our eyes in gentleness and understanding on which no shadow
falls. As the road of life we walk together lengthens, forbid
that the dust of it should ever drift into our souls. Help us to
have the sense to climb high places of memory and of imagination, so that we may remember the beauty that lies behind us
and believe in the beauty that lies before. Make us sure that
romance does not depend on time or place, but that daily it
may be renewed in the recognition of those larger possibilities
in one another which love itself creates. Teach us to remember
the little courtesies, to be swift to speak the grateful and happy
word, to believe rejoicingly in each other's best, and to face all
life bravely because we face it with united hearts. So may whatever spot of earth thou givest us to dwell in be as a garden in
which all sweet and lovely things may grow; through Jesus
Christ our Lord.

WALTER RUSSELL BOWIE

FAMILY LIFE   211

Almighty God, heavenly Father, who seest our families and the
homes in which thy people dwell: Deliver us, we beseech thee,
from vain-glory, selfish pride, and every cause of bitterness.
Endue us with faith, temperance, and patience. Knit together
in true affection those who in holy wedlock have been made
one flesh. Turn the heart of the parents to their children, and
the heart of the children to their parents, in mutual respect and
love, and make us kindly affectioned one to another in the spirit
of thy blessed Son, our Saviour Jesus Christ.

Book of Common Prayer (USA)

BEFORE LISTENING   212

Help me, O God, to listen to this thy child, to hear what is
said and what is unsaid. Help me to be fair-minded, honest,
just, and loving, that the truth may be spoken and received;
through Jesus Christ our Lord.

                                        ROBERT N. RODENMAYER

THOSE WHO ARE DEAR TO US   213

Almighty Father, gracious and merciful, who keepest watch
above thine own: So fill our hearts with trust in thee, that by
night and by day, at all times and in all seasons, we may without fear commit those who are dear to us to thy never-failing
love, for this life and the life to come; through Christ our Lord.

                                        A Book of Simple Prayers

CHARITY IN MY OWN HOME   214

Accompany me today, O Spirit invisible, in all my goings, but
stay with me also when I am in my own home and among my
kindred. Forbid that I should fail to show to those nearest to
me the sympathy and consideration which thy grace enables me
to show to others with whom I have to do. Forbid that I
should refuse to my own household the courtesy and politeness
which I think proper to show to strangers. Let charity today
begin at home.

    Leave me not, O gracious Presence, in such hours as I may
today devote to the reading of books or of newspapers. Guide
my mind to choose the right books and, having chosen them,
to read them in the right way. When I read for profit, grant
that all I read may lead me nearer to thyself. When I read for
recreation, grant that what I read may not lead me away from
thee. Let all my reading so refresh my mind that I may the
more eagerly seek after whatsoever things are pure and fair and
true.

                                        JOHN BAILLIE

ABSENT LOVED ONES   215

For our absent loved ones we implore thy loving-kindness.
Keep them in life, keep them in growing honor; and for us,
grant that we remain worthy of their love. For Christ's sake,
let not our beloved blush for us, nor we for them. Grant us but
that, and grant us courage to endure lesser ills unshaken, and to
accept death, loss, and disappointment as it were straws upon
the tide of life.

ROBERT LOUIS STEVENSON

BOUND TOGETHER BY GOD'S LOVE   216

O God, whose fatherly care reacheth to the uttermost parts of
the earth: We humbly beseech thee graciously to behold and
bless those whom we love, now absent from us. Defend them
from all dangers of soul and body; and grant that both they and
we, drawing nearer to thee, may be bound together by thy love
in the communion of thy Holy Spirit, and in the fellowship of
thy saints; through Jesus Christ our Lord.

Book of Common Prayer (USA)

LOVE'S WIDE CIRCLE   217

Behold the homes wherein thy people dwell, O Lord, and let
peace and true joy abide therein. Keep far from us such things
as would hurt or harm our dear ones; and may the circle of our
love be wide enough to include all with whom we have any
relationship; for Christ's sake.

KENDIG BRUBAKER CULLY

WITH LAMPS TRIMMED   218
AND CANDLES LIGHTED

We thank thee, O God, for thy Son Jesus Christ, who is the
Treasure of our wisdom and knowledge. Help us, we pray thee,
to keep our lamps trimmed and our candles lighted, that we
may see our work and service for God and Christ and have
blessings from above, as the holy men and women had in the
days of old. Grant that we may let all things be done in peace
and love, in the Name and power of Jesus; and may all con-
descend to one another in meekness, patience, and quietness in
the fear of the Lord, being all ordered with the wisdom which
is from above; that our hearts, minds, and souls may be knit
together in the love of Christ, so that in him we may be all of
one mind and spirit. And whatever we do, grant that by thy
grace it be done in the Name and power of Jesus, to the glory of
God the Father who created all, and takes care of all, Blessed
for ever and ever.

GEORGE FOX

THE BOND OF PEACE   °219

O Lord, who hast taught us that without charity all our doings
are worth nothing: Send thy Holy Ghost, and pour into our
hearts that most excellent gift, the very bond of peace and of
all virtues, without which though we live, yet are we counted
dead before thee; for the sake of thine only Son, our Saviour
Jesus Christ.

Book of Common Prayer (USA)

THE PRECIOUS GIFT °220

O God, who hast taught us that without love all our good deeds amount to nothing: Grant us, we pray thee, this precious gift, that we may be freed from possessiveness and self-importance and all unseemly thoughts. So shall we come at last truly to know thee, who art love, even as we are known of thee; who with thy Son and the Holy Spirit we worship as one God, world without end.

J. W. S.

THE SPIRIT OF NEIGHBORLINESS 221

Increase, O God, the spirit of neighborliness among us; that in peril we may uphold one another, in calamity serve one another, in suffering tend one another, and in homelessness, loneliness, or exile befriend one another; through Jesus Christ our Lord.

ENGLISH SHELTER PRAYER

A NEW COMMANDMENT 222

O God of love, who hast given a new commandment, that we should love one another even as thou didst love us, the unworthy and the wandering, and gavest thy beloved Son for our life and salvation: Give to thy servants, in all time of our life on earth, a mind forgetful of past ill-will, a pure conscience and sincere thoughts, and a heart to love our brethren; through Jesus Christ our Lord.

Book of Common Order
(CHURCH OF SCOTLAND)

THIS IS OUR POVERTY   223

This is our poverty—
    That we do not belong to each other
    Nor serve one another.
    We go each his own way
    And do not care for our neighbor.
We pray thee, O Lord,
    Redeem us from this estrangement,
    Redeem us out of this loneliness.
    Deliver from the sin that divides us.
    Join us closely in true love.
    Have mercy upon all thy children.

                    The Church in Germany in Prayer

FOR HIS CHILDREN'S SAKE   °224

Most compassionate God, who bearest upon thy heart the suffering of thy children, and longest that we should permit thee to give us healing and peace; we thank thee for thy Son who ministered to weaknesses of body as well as to corruption of soul, through whom thou gavest to stricken men and women health of body, mind, and spirit. Grant us his utter faith in thee, that in the face of life's trials and perplexities we may share his trustful, confident mind, and be freed from the cares which destroy us. Grant us his devotion to thy kingdom, that we may be lifted out of ourselves, and find our strength renewed as we use to the utmost the powers thou hast given us. Grant us his unfaltering belief in thy goodness, that whether pain or joy be our lot, we may still know ourselves to be upheld by thine encompassing strength, and in that knowledge find rest. Most of all we pray for his spirit of service, that what thou givest us of health and strength may be returned to thee in work well done for thy children's sake, and all our powers and gifts be dedicated to thee, their Author, even as we have seen life poured out for us through the Cross of Jesus Christ.

                    MORGAN PHELPS NOYES

OUR USE OF THIS WORLD'S GOODS 225

Almighty God, whose loving hand hath given us all that we possess: Give us also grace to honor thee with our substance, remembering the account we must one day give as faithful stewards of thy bounty; for the sake of Jesus Christ our Lord.

Book of Common Prayer (USA)

THE LURE OF POMP AND PRIDE 226

O God, we who dwell so precariously in the midst of life and death pray thee to guard us against the lure of pomp and pride, and to keep our souls free from the false pretensions of power by which we seek to grow great in our own eyes. Thou, who in thy great glory didst humble thyself to be of no reputation, bring us back from every far country of ambition and prestige to weigh our lives in the balance of eternity, that we be not deceived. In all such moments make plain to us the victory of a modest meekness wherein life itself is crowned, but not by the hand of might.

SAMUEL H. MILLER

REBUKE OUR VIOLENCE 227

O Christ, at whose word the wind and waves of the sea were stilled: Rebuke, we pray thee, the noisy violence of men, that they may usher in the day of brotherhood and peace, when all may truly serve thee; who with the Father and the Holy Spirit livest and workest for us unceasingly, world without end.

The Grey Book

WISDOM   228

God grant me—
The serenity to accept the things I cannot change,
The courage to change the things I can,
And the wisdom to distinguish the one from the other.

REINHOLD NIEBUHR

WILLINGNESS TO LEARN   229

Lord Jesus Christ, who sat lowly in the midst of learned
men, both hearing them and asking them questions: Give unto
us that humility of heart, and willingness to learn, without
which no one can grow in wisdom; for the honor of thy holy
Name.

ERIC MILNER-WHITE *and* G. W. BRIGGS

TO PRIZE WHAT IS PRECIOUS   230

Grant us, O Lord, to know that which is worth knowing, to
love that which is worth loving, to praise what can bear with
praise, to hate what in thy sight is unworthy, to prize what to
thee is precious; and above all to search out and do what is well-
pleasing unto thee, through Christ our Lord.

THOMAS À KEMPIS

DETACHMENT   231

Grant us, O God, the true spirit of detachment, that we may
neither become enslaved by our possessions, nor entangled in
any interests we cannot consecrate to thee; through Christ our
Lord.

The Grey Book

TO CHOOSE WISELY 232

O Christ, I am young and the world is before me and I could do many things. Help me to choose wisely where I should go and what I should do. Help me to see where I may serve thee best. Let me see what my talents are and what is merely pride or dreams. And O Christ, let me never follow a path that leads away from thee!

AVERY BROOKE

YES OR NO 233

O God, who in many times and places hast asked a question of thy chosen ones: Grant us grace so to hear thy voice and to respond, that being obedient unto thee we may face an hour of decision and answer yes or no as thou would have us.

IRIS V. CULLY

KNOWLEDGE AND POWER 234

O Lord, we beseech thee mercifully to receive the prayers of thy people who call upon thee; and grant that we may both perceive and know what things we ought to do, and also have grace and power faithfully to fulfil the same; through Jesus Christ our Lord.

Book of Common Prayer (USA)

TO ADMIRE GREAT THINGS GREATLY 235

Give me, O Lord, inward gravity of soul, that I may attain to a deeper sense of thy presence; that when I speak of thee I may attest and strengthen my reverence by my outward bearing. Help me to admire great things greatly, and never to belittle by jest or criticism anything that may help others.

L. H. M. SOULSBY

JOY IN OTHERS' HAPPINESS 236

O God, the wind of whose Spirit bloweth where it listeth, and whose rain falleth where it will: Quicken our ears to hear and our eyes to see the signs of thy presence, not only where our habits and conventions expect them, but wherever thy bounty bestows them. So shall our lives be gladdened by every miracle of grace, and our wills be alert to praise thy goodness to every creature; for his Name's sake who was born of the Spirit, the only Saviour of the world.

Prayers of the Spirit

DELIGHT IN SIMPLE THINGS 237

O God, who hast made the heaven and the earth and all that is good and lovely, and in thy blessed Son hast shown us that the secret of joy is a heart free from selfish desire: Help us to delight in simple things, and to rejoice in the beauties which abound in thy creation; through the same Jesus Christ our Lord.

UNKNOWN

DRY PLACES MADE GREEN 238

O God, whose love is our life: Open our hearts, we beseech thee, to receive thy gifts. Take away our coldness and calculation, the blindness of pride, and the luxury of hurt feelings; and so pour out upon us thy quickening Spirit that our dry places may be green again, and our whole being rejoice in thee; through Jesus Christ our Lord.

ROBERT N. RODENMAYER

NO SMALL IMAGINATIONS 239

Ennoble my soul, O God, with such love of thee that no self-seeking will debase my words or deeds, no small imaginations demean my thoughts. And help me so to arrange my time and spend my energies in work proportionable to the dignity of a disciple of Christ, that I may serve my generation with the powers which thou hast graciously bestowed; for thy Name's sake.

L. H. M. SOULSBY

THE GIFT OF FAITH 240

O heavenly Father, who understandest all thy children: Bestow upon us, we beseech thee, thy gift of faith, that we may bring our perplexities to the light of thy wisdom, and receive the blessed encouragement of thy sympathy, and a clearer knowledge of thy will; through Christ our Lord.

A Book of Collects

COOLNESS AND CALM 241

O Holy Spirit, Giver of life, who in the beginning didst move upon the face of the deep: Spread abroad in our hearts, we pray thee, thy coolness and thy calm. Help us to be silent before we speak, and speaking, so to measure our words that they may not injure but heal, binding up what was broken and giving light where darkness reigned; through Jesus Christ our Lord.

J. W. S.

QUIET MY TONGUE 242

O Lord, when I know I am better than my friends at doing something, it seems stupid to pretend I'm not. But help me, O Lord, not to be too proud. Quiet my tongue when I would boast. Help me not to hurt the feelings of the person less good at it than I. Remind me how the loser feels, so I can know what to say or do to make him feel better.

AVERY BROOKE

THE GIFT OF SILENCE 243

O God, who knowest how often we sin against thee with our spoken words: Help us to consecrate our speech to thy service, and to give, when it is needed, the precious gift of silence, wherein our hearts may listen for thy voice—and then speak only as in thy Name, thou lover of souls.

A Book of Collects

WHAT I KEEP TO MYSELF 244

Help me, Lord, to keep my discouragements to myself. Let me not dim the brightness of anybody else's day. Let no gloom of mine be added to the shadows through which the people around me already grope. And what I keep to myself, let me finally cast upon thee, O Lord, and lose my darkness in thy light.

THEODORE PARKER FERRIS

SUNSHINE 245

O Lord, bless this household, and give us sweet reasonableness in all our dealings with one another. Keep us from unkind words and unkind silences, make us alert to understand the needs and feelings of others, and grant that living in thy presence we may bring sunshine into cloudy places.

L. H. M. SOULSBY

TRUE WORTH   246

Guard our hearts, O God, that we may foster in them only
what is of true worth. Guard our minds, that the false and
base may find there no resting-place, but that we may be open
to beauty and truth. Guard our lips, lest by careless or unclean
talk we desecrate thy Name or thy creation. And grant that our
lives may be single in thought and word and deed.

CHARLES T. WEBB

DUTIES GREAT AND SMALL   247

Give us grace, O Lord, to work while it is day, fulfilling diligently and patiently whatever duty thou appointest us; doing
small things in the day of small things, and great labors if thou
summonest us to any; rising and working, or sitting still and
suffering, according to thy word.

CHRISTINA G. ROSSETTI

BEYOND CONFORMITY   248

Almighty God, whose Son taught that the faithful discharge of
duty is not enough: Lest we become unprofitable servants, lead
us, we pray, beyond conformity into the creative fellowship of
true disciples of the same Jesus Christ our Lord.

J. W. S.

UNTO HIM   249

Enable us, O God, to do all things as unto thee; that small
things may be filled with greatness, and great things crowned
with humility; through Christ our Lord.

JOHN U. STEPHENS

WHAT IS WISE, WHAT IS FOOLISH 250

Almighty God, by thy Spirit teach us what is wise and what is foolish, what is noble and what is mean, what is eternal and what is passing. May we prefer goodness to greatness, worthiness to wealth, the doing of one good thing to the hearing of many great ones; rather to be of thine unknown known ones written in thy book of life, than to have our names written in a book of earthly flame. Let us walk in a world filled with the Spirit of God, filled with joy and peace in believing; through Jesus Christ our Lord.

GEORGE DAWSON

TO DESTROY THE USELESS 251

O God, who hast created all men, I come before thee with all my powers and my weaknesses, my inherited tendencies and temperament. I pray thee to bring to perfection those things which are well-pleasing in thy sight, and to give me grace at last to destroy, as thou will and when thou will, those which cannot be used in thy service; that in all things I may grow up into Christ, who liveth and reigneth with thee and the Holy Ghost, one God, blessed for evermore.

GILBERT C. BINYON

GOD'S GUIDING HAND 252

O Lord, who canst lead us by ways we know not, and in paths we do not choose; who dost guide us through joy and sorrow, through victory and defeat, beyond our understanding: Give us grace so to discern thy guiding hand in all things, that being neither lifted up in vanity by success, nor cast down in despair by failure, we may press forward with hope and put our trust in thee; for the honor of thy holy Name.

ERIC MILNER-WHITE *and* G. W. BRIGGS

TO ABOUND IN ALL GOOD WORKS 253

O Thou, who art the true Sun of the world, ever rising and never going down, who by thy most wholesome appearing and sight dost nourish and gladden all things in heaven and earth: We beseech thee mercifully to shine into our hearts, that the night and darkness of sin, and the mists of error on every side, being driven away by the brightness of thy shining within our hearts, we may all our life walk without stumbling, as in the day-time, and being pure and clean from the works of darkness may abound in all good works which thou hast prepared for us to walk in.

DESIDERIUS ERASMUS

TO SEE HIS IMAGE 254

Jesus, our Master and our Friend, who claimest our service through the needs of our neighbors: Grant us so to see thine image in all our fellow-creatures, that in serving mankind we may minister to thee; who livest and reignest with the Father and the Holy Spirit, ever one God, world without end.

GILBERT C. BINYON

A MEASURE OF HIS SPIRIT 255

O Lord Jesus Christ, give us such a measure of thy Spirit that we may be enabled to obey thy teaching: To pacify anger, to take part in pity, to moderate desire, to increase love, to put away sorrow, to cast away vain-glory; not to be vindictive, not to fear death; ever entrusting our spirit to immortal God, who with thee and the Holy Ghost liveth and reigneth world without end.

ST. APPOLONIUS

TO FULFILL OUR MISSION 256

O God our Father, we pray that thou show us clearly the heart of the kingdom of God. We do not protest even if our life is destined to lead to the Cross, or if the way leads to our losing our lives. We will march in the face of distress and contrary winds. Teach us how to dispense with unnecessary things. Let us go forward without fear of death in order to fulfill our mission simply, surely, and steadily. Reveal to us our station clearly, and strengthen us to teach and guide by our example all sick persons, and even those who are ruled by evil. We pray that thou find us worthy to work through us.

TOYOHIKO KAGAWA

WRONG WORRIES 257

O God, when I worry that people will not like the way I look, or speak, or act—help me to remember that they look at me a lot less than I think, but that you watch me always.

AVERY BROOKE

UNWORTHY FEARS 258

O God our Father, thou knowest how often we fail because we are afraid. We fear what men will do if we stand for the right. We fear what they will say. We fear that we shall not have the strength to go on even if we begin. Forgive our weakness. Help us to remember our Master and all that he endured for us, so that we may never be afraid of men, but only of sinning against thy love. We ask it in his Name.

A. G. PITE

FEAR OF DANGER 259

There is no storme but this
Of your owne Cowardise
That braves you out;
You are the storme that mocks
Yourselves, you are the rocks
Of your owne doubt.
Besides this feare of danger, ther's no danger here;
And he that here fears danger, does deserve his fear.

RICHARD CRASHAW

ADVERSARIES WITHOUT AND WITHIN 260

Almighty God, who knowest the strength and persistence of
our adversaries without and within: Help us to stand fast,
knowing that the same sufferings are required of our brotherhood throughout the world; and make us ever confident that
the God of all grace, having called us to eternal glory in Christ,
will make us whole and secure and strong.

J. W. S.

HEROIC LOVE 261

O Thou who art heroic love, keep alive in our hearts, we
beseech thee, that adventurous spirit which makes men scorn
the way of safety so that thy will be done. And help us to be
worthy of those courageous souls who in every age have risked
all in obedience to thee, and for whom the trumpets sounded
on the other side; through Jesus Christ our Lord.

The Grey Book

RIDING THE STORMS 262

Grant, almighty God, that in all our troubles we may look to thee, assured of thy mercy and loving-kindness; so that whatever this life may bring, the storms may pass over us and not shake the peace of God deep within us. Then, though we be troubled on every side, we shall not be crushed; if perplexed, we shall not be driven to despair; persecuted and even struck down, we shall not be destroyed—since we have what no man can take away, the faith that thou art our Father who lovest us. We ask in the Name of Jesus Christ, in whom we have light and life, now and forever.

Services for Broadcasting

FOR ADEQUACY 263

O God, come to us, we pray thee, with the resources of thy power, that we may be strong within. We ask not for easy lives, but for adequacy. We ask not to be freed from storms, but to build our houses on rock that will not fall. We pray not for a smooth sea, but for a stout ship, a good compass, and a strong heart; in the Name of him who faced enmity and death without flinching, thy Son Jesus Christ our Lord.

HARRY EMERSON FOSDICK

TO STAND FAST 264

Fortify us, O God, with the courage which comes only from thee; that in the midst of all our perils having done all, we may stand fast, knowing that thou art faithful; for Jesus Christ's sake.

Prayers of the Spirit

STAND AS PILLARS 265

Come to us, O Holy Ghost, Spirit of might, thou that foldest up the heavens as a curtain and shakest terribly the earth; come, strengthen us in the inner man; for if thou be with us, we cannot be moved; if thou be for us, who can be against us? Grant us the grace of final perseverance, that we may endure to the end, and so, overcoming by thy power, stand as pillars in the temple of our God.

A. H. STANTON

FOR VALOR 266

O Lord Christ, who in our very nature didst fight to win and labor to achieve: So clothe us with thy valor, that we, delivered from the fear of living as Christians, may attack the problems of our troubled day with serene mind and unconquerable will; for the honor of thy holy Name.

CHARLES HENRY BRENT

FIRM AND RESOLUTE 267

O Saviour, who didst set thy face steadfastly to go to Jerusalem to thy Cross and passion: Help us, thy weak and wavering disciples, to be firm and resolute in doing those things that lie before us. Help us to overcome difficulties and persevere in spite of failures. When we are weary and disheartened and ready to give in, do thou fill us with fresh courage and strength, and keep us faithful to our work; for thy Name's sake.

Book of Common Order
(CHURCH OF SCOTLAND)

TRUE COURAGE   268

O God, who through thy Son Jesus Christ hast promised a blessing to the meek upon the earth: Take from us all pride and vanity, boasting and forwardness, and give us the true courage that shows itself by gentleness, the true wisdom that shows itself by simplicity, and the true power that shows itself by modesty; for Christ's sake.

CHARLES KINGSLEY

FACING OPPOSITION   269

O Holy Spirit, grant us, we pray thee, the gift of courage. Enable us to live as Jesus lived, in steadfast opposition to sin and in courageous faith in the power of God. As he faced the hatred of enemies and the desertion of friends, so may we be prepared to face manfully whatever opposition or enmity our service of him may arouse against us, in certain hope that in all things we can be strengthened through him who has overcome the world, the same Jesus Christ our Lord.

E. M. VENABLES

IN THE BATTLE   270

Lord, I am no hero; I have been careless, cowardly, sometimes all but mutinous. Punishment I have deserved, I deny it not. But a traitor I have never been; a deserter I have never been. I have tried to fight on thy side in thy battle against evil. I have tried to do the duty which lay nearest me; and to leave whatever thou didst commit to my charge a little better than I found it. I have not been good, but at least I have tried to be good. Take the will for the deed, good Lord. Strike not my unworthy name off the roll-call, which is the blessed company of all faithful people, even though I stand lowest and last upon the list.

CHARLES KINGSLEY

COSTLY LOYALTY   271

Grant, O Lord, that in all our sufferings here upon earth for the
testimony of thy truth, we may steadfastly look up to heaven,
and by faith behold the glory that shall be revealed; and, being
filled with the Holy Ghost, may learn to love and bless our per-
secutors by the example of thy first Martyr Saint Stephen, who
prayed for his murderers to thee, O blessed Jesus, who standest
at the right hand of God to help all those who suffer for thee,
our only Mediator and Advocate.

Book of Common Prayer (USA)

MORE THAN CONQUERORS   272

O Jesus Christ, the Lord of all good life: Enrich and purify our
lives, we pray thee, and so deepen in us our discipleship that in
the power of thy Spirit we may reveal thy glory to others. We
do not ask thee to keep us safe but to keep us loyal to thee; who
for us faced death unafraid, and dost live and reign for ever
and ever.

The Grey Book

LOVE THAT REACHES OUT   °273

O God, we dedicate ourselves anew to thee and to thy service.
Pour into our hearts such a love for thee that we may truly love
our neighbors as ourselves—a love that leaps the boundaries of
race or color or creed or kind, that knows no distinction of class,
that reaches out a saving hand even unto the least of these our
brethren. Fill our lives with the single motive of service, and
use us, Lord, use us for thine own purposes, just as thou wilt,
and when, and where; through Christ our Master.

WILLIAM SCARLETT

RESOLUTE AND TRANQUIL   274

O Lord Jesus Christ, Son of the most high God, who didst
learn obedience by the things which thou didst suffer, even
unto death: Give us grace to do the will of our Father with an
obedience like thine, resolute and tranquil, instant and complete; for the honor of thy holy Name.

ERIC MILNER-WHITE and G. W. BRIGGS

A LITANY OF COURAGE   275

Be strong in the Lord,
And in the power of his might.
Let us pray.

Raise up, O Lord, thy power,
And come among us, and with great might strengthen us.

For all who have labored for freedom, sound government, and
just laws; and for those who gave their lives that truth and justice might live,
We praise thee, O Lord.

For those who have resisted falsehood and bribery,
We bless thy Name.

For all who, following the great traditions, have defied those
conventions which impede the coming of thy kingdom on
earth,
We thank thee, O God.

For those who though disappointed never lost heart,
O Lord, we praise thee.

For all who, unknown and unrewarded, lived for thee and for
their fellowmen,
We bless thy holy Name.

Raise up, O Lord, thy power,
And strengthen us by thy grace.

Uphold, O God, our loyalty to every righteous cause,
*That when we suffer for our fidelity, we may rejoice to find
our place in the citizenship of heaven.*

That we may grow in modesty and courtesy,
    We pray thee.
That when it is called for we may have the courage of gentleness,
    We beseech thee.
That toward our neighbor, as toward thee, we may be sincere in word and deed,
    O Lord, we pray thee.

Almighty Father, who callest us to build the City of God, deepen in us our discipleship, and make us ready for adventure. We do not ask that thou wilt keep us safe, but that thou wilt keep us loyal; for his sake, and in his Spirit, who faced death unafraid, our Saviour Jesus Christ.

Go forth into the world in peace; be of good courage; fight the good fight of faith; that you may finish your course with joy, and receive the blessing of God.

Chapel Services and Prayers

UNTO THE END   276

O Lord God, when thou givest us to endeavor any great matter, grant us also to know that it is not the beginning, but the continuing of the same until it be thoroughly finished, that yieldeth the true glory; through him who finished thy work with his life, our Saviour Jesus Christ.

SIR FRANCIS DRAKE

BE WITH US NOW   277

O holy Christ, O Lord of Light,
Succor me now in my affright.
O holy Christ, now in this hour
Keep tryst with me and be my Tower.

Ancient Gaelic Prayer

11

Praise and Thanksgiving

*O praise the Lord with me, and let us magnify
his Name together.*

PSALM 34:3

LET US DANCE BEFORE THEE °278

O God of peace and charity! we beseech thee, holy Lord,
almighty Father, eternal God, deliver us from all temptation,
give us help in every conflict, strengthen us in all tribulation.
Give us patience in adversity, grant that we may worship thee
with a pure heart, let us dance before thee with a clean conscience, let us serve thee with all our strength. We bless thee,
Holy Trinity, we give thanks to thee, we praise thee every day,
we pray unto thee "Abba, Father." May our praise be sweet to
thee and our prayer acceptable.

Gallican Sacramentary

OUR GUIDE AND FRIEND 279

We thank thee, Lord, that we have thy wisdom, lying at the
mercy of every seeking mind; O thou most wonderful in the
realm of truth!

We thank thee, Lord, that we have thy world, river and sea,
hill and valley, forest and field, for our dwelling; O thou most
glorious in the realm of beauty!

We thank thee, Lord, that we have thyself, for our guide
and friend; O thou most faithful in the realm of love!

Thanks be to thee for thine unspeakable gifts.

A. S. T. FISHER

SPECIAL TOKENS   280

Father of lights, from whose unshadowed home above comes every good and perfect gift, I receive as from thy hand my share in the common blessings which, without respect of persons, hourly descend upon mankind. I thank thee also for the special tokens of thy friendship and personal care that have made me glad. Help me to use these and all thy bounties according to thy design, that my whole life may be a hymn of praise to thee; through Jesus Christ our Lord.

CHARLES HENRY BRENT

COMPOSURE AND SILENCE   281

He has created the world
And bears it with great strength.
He creates all things daily anew
By his mighty word.
He rules through the ages
And fills the years with his fruit.
He gives the seed and gives the harvest,
He gives the work and blesses the deed.
In grief he refreshes with great joy.
Amidst the restlessness he calls us with holy calling
To composure and silence.
We adore him.

The Church in Germany in Prayer

SENSITIVE TO GRACE   282

O Holy Spirit, splendor of God, keep us sensitive to the grace that is round about us.

Let not the needs of our neighbors, from being so familiar, suffer from our neglect, nor the virtues of our friends, from continual proof of them, go quite unblessed; but as thou givest us our daily bread, give us also daily thankfulness; for the love of our Lord Jesus Christ.

A. S. T. FISHER

HIS COMPANIONSHIP ALL THE WAY 283

Most gracious God, who hast made us stewards of thy bounty, and trusted us with the use of thy gifts: We lift our hearts in thanksgiving for the manifold tokens of thy surrounding love. We thank thee for life, and the joy of it; for health, and all the powers with which thou hast endowed us; for the wondrous world about us; for the greater world within us, and every gleam of light which turns our minds towards thee; for the love of friends and kindred, and their belief in us; for the way over which we have come, and all that has been good in it; for the way that lies untrodden before us, and our chance to make it the way of peace and righteousness; for thy companionship all the way, and our assurance that thou wilt guide our steps aright. For all that thou art to us, and all that we may be to thee, we give thanks unto thee, the Author of goodness, and bless thy name for thy mercies which endure throughout all generations.

MORGAN PHELPS NOYES

BEAUTY AND MAJESTY 284

O Thou, who hast created all things, and for whose glory they are and were created, we thank thee for the beauty of this world: the glory of leaf and flower, the majesty and mystery of stars, the singing of birds, the splendors of dawn and sunset. Glorious as are thy manifestations in nature, thou thyself art yet more glorious. Awe us by thy holiness, subdue us by thy majesty; yet in the tenderness of thy grace cause us to stand before thee confident and unashamed, that when we hear thy voice saying, "Whom shall I send and who will go for us?" our hearts will make reply, "Here are we, Lord, send us!"

SAMUEL MCCOMB

Now unto thee, O heavenly Father, be all praise and glory that day by day thou dost richly fill my life with various blessings—

A home to share, kindred to love, and friends to cherish:
A place to fill and a work to do:
A green world to live in, blue skies above me, and pure air to breathe:
Healthy exercise and simple pleasures:
My race's long history to remember and its great men to follow:
Good books to read and many arts and crafts to delight in:
So much that is worth knowing and the skill and science to know it:
Those high thoughts that sometimes fill my mind and come I know not whence:
Many happy days, and that inward calm that thou givest me in days of gloom:
The peace, passing understanding, that comes from thine indwelling in my soul:
The faith that looks through death, and the hope of a larger life beyond the grave.

I thank thee, O Lord God, that though with liberal hand thou hast at all times showered thy blessings upon our human kind, yet in Jesus Christ thou hast done greater things for us than thou ever didst before—

Making home sweeter and friends dearer:
Turning sorrow into gladness and pain into the soul's victory:
Robbing death of its sting:
Robbing sin of its power:
Making peace more peaceful and joy more joyful and faith and hope more secure.

JOHN BAILLIE

WE LOOK UP 286

We look up
To his glory and majesty.
He stands in the midst,
He the beginning and the end.
Ever again he meets us.
He reveals himself
In the wonder of the crystal,
In the flower,
In beast,
And in man.
Upon all his works rests the splendor of his Name.
Lord, keep our hearts open
And our eyes clear
To discern the traces of thy work.
Let us ever be awake
To receive thy messengers.
We praise thee!

The Church in Germany in Prayer

THE UNSEARCHABLE RICHES OF GOD 287

Lord God, Eternal, Immortal, Invisible, the mysteries of whose being are unsearchable: We bless thee for the revelation which thou hast made of thyself as Father, Son, and Holy Spirit. Grant, we pray thee, that holding fast to our faith we may magnify thy glorious Name, and with joy and reverence walk as in thy presence who art one God, world without end.

Scottish Book of Common Prayer
(EPISCOPAL CHURCH IN SCOTLAND)

RARE MOMENTS OF JOY AND RENEWAL 288

We give thee thanks, O God,

For great moments of joy and strength that come to us when by a strong and special movement of grace we are able to perform some act of pure and disinterested love.

For the clean fire of that love which floods the soul and cleanses the whole man and leaves us filled with an unexpected lightness and freedom for action.

For the moment of pure prayer which not only establishes order in the soul, but even fortifies us against physical weariness and brings us a new lease on life itself.

Glory be to thee for thy precious gift!

THOMAS MERTON

ROBED IN MAJESTY °289

The Lord reigns as king, robed in majesty; royalty the Lord has for robe and girdle. He it was that founded the solid earth, to abide immovable. Firm stood thy throne ere ever the world began; from all eternity, thou art. Loud the rivers echo, Lord, loud the rivers echo, crashing down in flood. Magnificent the roar of eddying waters; magnificent the sea's rage; magnificent above these, the Lord reigns in heaven. How faithful, Lord, are thy promises! Holy is thy house, and must needs be holy until the end of time.

RONALD KNOX

HIS RESPLENDENT GLORY 290

Christ, holy and strong, in whom all human possibilities are fulfilled, and all the treasuries of God stand revealed: Receive, we pray thee, the adoration of thy people. Above our failure and bewilderment, our sins, ignorances, and anxieties, we lift our hearts to thy perfection in love and reverence, beseeching thee to manifest thyself to the world which waits for thee as for the dawn. Rise upon us, O Lord, in thy resplendent glory, and lighten for us the way that we should walk in; for thy sake who dost live and govern all things, world without end.

The Grey Book

ALL HIS GOODNESS 291

Heavenly Father, for all thy goodness to us, we bless and praise thy holy Name:

For the beauty of this good earth, for the loveliness of flowers and changing seasons, for trees in winter darkly etched against a steel-gray sky, for racing clouds and starry nights:

For our friends and all the friendliness which has blessed our lives:

For human love which admits us so intimately into thy divine presence:

For life itself with all its glory, its challenge, its opportunity.

Keep us close to thee, we pray thee, that none of life be wasted; and make us channels and agents of thy good will in a troubled world.

WILLIAM SCARLETT

THANKSGIVING FOR VARIED GIFTS   292

We come to thee, O God, with words of thanksgiving on our lips. We thank thee for thy gifts. They are as varied as our needs, as manifold as our desires. Our hearts cry for love, and thou hast given us the love of parent and of friend, that have been as thy benediction on our lives. Our minds crave light and knowledge, and thy Spirit hath kindled a lamp within us. We long for the vision of beauty, and thou hast revealed thyself gloriously in the open page of nature. May we take these gifts, not for their own sake only, but as steps by which to mount upward to thee, who art the perfection of love and truth and beauty.

SAMUEL MCCOMB

BLESSINGS MULTIPLIED   293

For the benison of sunshine, and the beauty of rain;
For birdsong at morning and starshine at night;
For good and many-tasting food, for the great gift of sleep;
For the discoveries of science, and the heritage of art;
For the ministry of books, and for music, beyond the reach of
    words;
For the care of fathers and mothers, and the happiness of home;
For the sanity of friendship, and the madness of love;
Thanks be to the Lord our God.

A. S. T. FISHER

SO FREELY BESTOWED 294

O Merciful Father, we humbly thank thee for all thy gifts so freely bestowed upon us: For life and health, for power to work and leisure to rest, and for all that is beautiful in creation and in the lives of men. Above all, we praise thee for opportunities to grow in grace in the fellowship of the Holy Spirit, beseeching thee to fill our hearts with all joy and peace in believing; for his sake who came that we might have life more abundant, thy Son Jesus Christ our Lord.

Book of Common Prayer
(ANGLICAN CHURCH OF CANADA)

ALL THE GOOD GIFTS 295

O God, who art near us always, we would speak with thee and thank thee for all the good gifts with which thou hast filled our lives: For love that makes life beautiful, for all thoughts that uplift and gladden us, for disappointment and failure which humble us, for pain and distress which teach us our need; but most of all for our hope in thee, and the fulness of joy which thy presence brings. We all wish to serve thee. Show to each of us how we may do it best—hands to work for thee, feet to run for thee, lips to speak of thee, thoughts to use for thee, hearts to love as thou lovest. This we ask in thy strength, and for the sake of Jesus Christ our Lord.

A Book of Simple Prayers

THOSE WHO MEAN SO MUCH °296

We give thee thanks, O God, for those who mean so much to us—

Those to whom we can go at any time.

Those with whom we can talk and keep nothing back, knowing that they will not laugh at our dreams or our failures.

Those in whose presence it is easier to be good.

Those who by their warning have held us back from mistakes we might have made.

Above all, we thank thee for Jesus Christ, Lord of our hearts and Saviour of our souls, in whose Name we offer this thanksgiving.

WILLIAM BARCLAY

SIGNS OF HOPE 297

We thank thee, Lord
That however hopeless our work may seem,
However dark the night around us,
However meagre the response to thy Spirit,
Still thou hast ordained for us a hope.
We thank thee that we can never despair
Because we know, past all doubting,
That here and there in this world thy kingdom has already
    come,
Thy will has already begun to rule.
We thank thee that here and there are homes made beautiful by
    thy presence,
Lives lived purely and faithfully for thee,
Children and child-like souls whose clear and simple trust
Brings thee thyself down amongst men.

J. S. HOYLAND

THOSE WHO HELPED US   298

O God, we thank thee for those who strengthened us when we were weak, raised us up when we were cast down, and comforted us when we knew not ourselves. Help us now to strengthen the weak, raise up the fallen, and forgive those who know not what they do; walking humbly with them as followers of thy Son, our Saviour Jesus Christ.

A. E. S.

THE WISE OF EVERY LAND   299

Almighty God, before whom stand the spirits of the living and the dead, and who livest in all pure and humble and gracious souls: We thank thee for the wise of every land and nation, all faithful teachers of mankind, and all who have sought to bless men by their service and to bring light to the dark places of the earth. All glory, honor, and power be unto thee, O Father, now and forever.

The Grey Book

MELODY IN OUR HEARTS   300

Forbid, O God, that we thy children allow ourselves to be carried away by fair speeches. Help us to have hold of the truth in ourselves, and of the life and light and power of the Most High, knowing Christ to be our Bread of Life, and singing in the Spirit, making melody in our hearts to the Lord; to whom be glory everlasting.

GEORGE FOX

SAINTS IN EVERYDAY LIFE 301

We thank thee, Lord, for saints in everyday life: men and women of prayer who have borne suffering for noble ends without complaint and without display, and all who have endured pain with patience and purity of life, in the strength of him who for the joy that was set before him endured the Cross; even our Saviour Jesus Christ.

UNKNOWN

FOR TRUE PROGRESS °302

We beseech thee, good God, lover of men, to look upon our prayer and to cleanse our souls and bodies. Grant, O God, to those who pray with us, progress in life and in faith and in spiritual understanding; so that always guarded by thy might, we may send up glory to thee the Father, and to the Son, and to the Holy Spirit, now and forever and for ages of ages.

Liturgy of St. John Chrysostom

FOR LIFE ITSELF 303

O God, I thank thee for my life. I thank thee for my body, for the strength of my limbs, and for my mind. I thank thee for my soul, for the perception that feels thee near to me and knows that my body is even now the temple of thy Holy Spirit.

I thank thee for my surroundings, for the fresh air and the sweet earth, and the love of friends. I thank thee also for my pains and difficulties, both of body and of soul, because they are the means whereby I shall attain to a clearer light and truer understanding. Above all, I thank thee for the life and death of thy holy Son, through whom by thy power I am brought to peace.

J. LESLIE JOHNSTON

GIFTS OF NATURE AND OF GRACE   304

Almighty God, Father of all mercies, we thank thee for all thou hast given, and for all thou hast forgiven us. We thank thee for thy hidden blessings, and for those which in our negligence we have passed over; for every gift of nature or of grace; for the power of loving; for all thou hast yet in store for us for everything, whether joy or sorrow, whereby thou art drawing us to thyself; through Jesus Christ our Lord.

ST. PAUL'S CATHEDRAL, BOSTON

WE THANK THEE FOR OUR SENSES   305

O God, we thank thee for this universe, our great home; for its vastness and its riches, and for the manifoldness of the life which teems upon it and of which we are a part. We praise thee for the arching sky and the blessed winds, for the driving clouds and the constellations on high. We praise thee for the salt sea and the running water, for the everlasting hills, for the trees, and for the grass under our feet. We thank thee for our senses by which we can see the splendor of the morning, and hear the jubilant songs of love, the smell of breath of the springtime. Grant us, we pray thee, a heart wide open to all this beauty, and save our souls from being so steeped in care or so darkened by passion that we pass heedless and unseeing when even the thornbush by the wayside is aflame with the glory of God.

WALTER RAUSCHENBUSCH

A LITANY OF THANKSGIVING   306

Almighty God, our heavenly Father, from whom cometh every good and perfect gift, we call to remembrance thy loving kindness and thy tender mercies which have been ever of old, and with grateful hearts we lift up to thee the voice of our thanksgiving.

For all the gifts which thou hast bestowed upon us; for the life thou hast given us, and the world in which we live:
We praise thee, O God.
For the work we are enabled to do, and the truth we are permitted to learn; for whatever of good there has been in our past lives, and for all the hopes and aspirations which lead us on toward better things:
We praise thee.
For the order and constancy of nature; for the beauty and bounty of the world; for day and night, summer and winter, seed-time and harvest; for the varied gifts of loveliness and use which every season brings:
We praise thee.
For all the comforts and gladness of life; for our homes and all our home-blessings; for our friends and all the pure pleasures of social intercourse; for the love, sympathy, and goodwill of men:
We praise thee, O God.
For education, and all the privileges we enjoy through literature, science, and art; for the help and counsel of those who are wiser and better than ourselves:
We praise thee, O God.
For Prophets and Apostles, and all earnest seekers after truth; for all lovers and helpers of mankind, and all godly and gifted men and women:
We praise thee.
For the gift of thy Son Jesus Christ, and all the helps and hopes which are ours as his disciples; for the presence and inspiration of thy Holy Spirit, and for all the ministries of thy truth and grace:
We praise thee.

For communion with thee, the Father of our spirits; for the light and peace that are gained through trust and obedience, and the darkness and disquietude which befall us when we disobey thy laws and follow our lower desires and selfish passions:

We praise thee, O God.

For the desire and power to help others; for every opportunity of serving our generation according to thy will, and manifesting the grace of Christ to men:

We praise thee, O God.

For all the discipline of life; for the tasks and trials by which we are trained to patience, self-knowledge, and self-conquest, and brought into closer sympathy with our suffering brethren, for troubles which have lifted us nearer thee and drawn us into deeper fellowship with Jesus Christ:

We praise thee.

For the sacred and tender ties which bind us to the unseen world; for the faith which dispels the shadows of earth, and fills the saddest and the lost moments of life with the light of an immortal hope:

We praise thee.

God of all grace and love, we have praised thee with our lips: grant that we may also praise thee in consecrated and faithful lives. And may the words of our mouth and the meditations of our heart be acceptable in thy sight, O Lord, our Strength and our Redeemer.

JOHN HUNTER

THE MARVEL OF CREATION 307

O God, Creator and Father, we praise thee for the marvel of beauty in which thou hast set our lives. We bless thee for thy love, new every morning, shedding upon us the life-giving power of thy holiness. May we never accept as commonplace the mystery of creation, but let thy majesty flood our souls and wash away all that is mean and sordid; that whatever work our hands find to do may be done to thy honor and glory, and for the sake of Jesus Christ our Lord.

New Every Morning

SONG OF ADORATION   308

We praise thee, we worship thee,
We adore thee.
Thou holdest the heavens in thy hand,
All stars rejoice in thy glory.
Thou comest in the sunrise and the song of morn
And blessest in the splendor of the noonday.
The stars in their courses magnify thee,
Day and night tell of thy glory.
Thy peace blows over the earth
And the breath of thy mouth fills all space.
Thy voice comes in the thunder of the storm
And the song of the wind whispers of thy majesty.
Thou satisfiest all things living with thine abundance
And our hearts bow at thy presence.
Accept us, thy children, Eternal Father,
And hearken to our prayer.
Bend over us, Eternal Love,
And bless us.

The Church in Germany in Prayer

THE GREAT WORKS OF HIS HANDS   °309

We magnify thee, O Lord almighty, we bless the excellency of
thy name in the great works of thy hands, the manifold beauties of earth and sky and sea, the courses of the stars and light,
the songs of birds, the hues of flowers, the diversity of all living
creatures, and, upholding all, thy wisdom, marvellous worthy to
be praised; but most, that by thy sure promise we now do only
taste the glory that shall be revealed, when thou, O God, wilt
take the power and reign; world without end.

Book of Common Prayer
(CHURCH OF INDIA, PAKISTAN, BURMA, AND CEYLON)

MIND AND HEART REJOICE IN CREATION 310

Creator Spirit, who broodest everlastingly over the lands and waters of earth, enduing them with forms and colors which no human skill can copy; give me today, I beseech thee, the mind and heart to rejoice in thy creation.

Forbid that I should walk through thy beautiful world with unseeing eyes:

Forbid that the lure of the market-place should ever entirely steal my heart away from the love of the open acres and the green trees:

Forbid that under the low roof of workshop or office or study I should ever forget thy great overarching sky:

Forbid that when all thy creatures are greeting the morning with songs and shouts of joy, I alone should wear a dull and sullen face.

Let the energy and vigor which in thy wisdom thou hast infused into every living thing stir today within my being, that I may not be among the creatures as a sluggard and a drone:

And above all give me grace to use these beauties of earth without me, and this eager stirring of life within me, as means whereby my soul may rise from creature to Creator, and from nature to nature's God.

JOHN BAILLIE

FRUITS OF THE EARTH   311

We entreat thee, O Lord, mercifully to bless the air and the dews, the rains and the winds; that through thy heavenly benediction all may be saved from dearth and famine, and enjoy the fruits of the earth in abundance and plenty; for the eyes of all wait upon thee, O Lord, who givest them their meat in due season.

The Eucharist in India

JOY IN GOD'S CREATION   312

O heavenly Father, who hast filled the world with beauty:
Open, we beseech thee, our eyes to behold thy gracious hand in
all thy works, that rejoicing in thy whole creation, we may learn
to serve thee with gladness; for the sake of him through whom
all things were made, thy Son Jesus Christ our Lord.

Book of Common Prayer (USA)

THE EVER PRESENT CHRIST   313

Come thou, O Christ, lover of our race, and reign among us
in love and joy and peace. Extend thy empire over human
hearts; let the burning vision of thy beauty shine out clear before the eyes of the world; and hasten the consummation of thy
kingdom in which love shall be the only king: that the love
wherewith the Father loves thee may be in us, and we be one
in thee; to whom be blessing and honor for ever and ever.

The Grey Book

THE WONDER OF THE WORLD   314

We rejoice, O God, in the wonder of the world and the beauty
of the earth; the discoveries of science and the treasures of art;
the power of music and the wealth of literature; the faculty of
seeing and hearing, in body and in spirit. We rejoice in all
things that make us one with thee in thy eternal joy, beseeching
thee for grace to grow toward the fulfilment of the hope thou
hast for us, as revealed in thy Son, our Saviour Jesus Christ.

Services for Broadcasting

PRAISE TO THE LORD °315

Praise to the Lord, the Almighty, the King of creation;
O my soul praise him, for he is thy health and salvation;
Join the great throng, psaltery, organ, and song,
      Sounding in glad adoration.
Praise to the Lord, who doth prosper thy way and defend thee;
Surely his goodness and mercy shall ever attend thee;
Ponder anew what the Almighty can do,
      Who with his love doth befriend thee.

                    JOACHIM NEANDER

FELLOWSHIP IN CHRIST 316

Eternal God, our heavenly Father, who didst come in Jesus
Christ to show forth thy love to the world; we praise and bless
thee for the Church, through which thou dost continue thy
work for us men and for our salvation. We praise thee for a
fellowship in Christ that knows no barrier of land or sea but
joins together a great multitude, from all nations and kindreds
and tongues, in the bonds of a common faith and devotion.
Grant us grace to commit ourselves wholly to thee, that we
may come to newness of life; and that, belonging to the company of thy faithful servants, we may be used of thee for the
extension of thy kingdom upon earth; through Jesus Christ our
Lord.

                    ERNEST F. TITTLE

12

The Life of Prayer

*Right relation between prayer and conduct is not that
conduct is supremely important and prayer may help it, but
that prayer is supremely important and conduct tests it.*

WILLIAM TEMPLE

THE SPIRIT OF PRAYER °317

O Almighty God, from whom every good prayer cometh, and
who pourest out on all who desire it the Spirit of grace and supplications: Deliver us, when we draw nigh to thee, from coldness of heart and wanderings of mind; that with steadfast
thoughts and kindled affections we may worship thee in spirit
and in truth; through Jesus Christ our Lord.

WILLIAM BRIGHT

WITH A PURE HEART 318

O Lord our God, great, eternal, wonderful in glory, who keepest covenant and promises with those that love thee with their
whole heart; who art the life of all, the help of those who flee
unto thee, the hope of all who cry unto thee: Cleanse us from
our sins, and from every thought displeasing to thy goodness;
that with a pure heart and a clear soul, with perfect love and
calm hope, we may venture confidently and fearlessly to pray
unto thee.

WILLIAM BRIGHT

PRAYERS BETTER THAN OUR OWN   319

O Holy Spirit, Giver of light and life: Impart to us, we pray
thee, thoughts higher than our own thoughts, prayers better
than our own prayers, and powers beyond our own; that we may
spend and be spent in the ways of love and goodness, after the
perfect image of our Saviour, Jesus Christ.

ERIC MILNER-WHITE *and* G. W. BRIGGS

JESUS THE GREAT HIGH PRIEST   °320

Most gracious Father, whose Son shared fully in all our experience of temptation, except that he never sinned: Grant that
by the intercession of our great High Priest, who has entered
the inmost heaven, we may approach the throne of grace with
fullest confidence, and receive mercy for our failures, and grace
to help in time of need; through the same Jesus Christ our
Lord.

J. W. S.

PRAY THOU THYSELF IN ME   321

O Lord, I know not what to ask of thee. Thou alone knowest
my true needs. Thou lovest me more than I myself know how
to love. I dare not ask either a cross or consolation: I can only
wait on thee. My heart is open to thee. Visit and help me, for
thy great mercy's sake. Strike me and heal me, cast me down
and raise me up. I worship in silence thy holy will and thine
inscrutable ways, and offer myself as a sacrifice to thee. I put all
my trust in thee. I have no other desire than to fulfil thy will.
Teach me how to pray. Pray thou thyself in me.

METROPOLITAN PHILARET OF MOSCOW

THE SPIRIT OF WISDOM   °322

O God, by whom the humble-minded are guided in judgment, and light riseth up in darkness for the faithful: Grant us in all our doubts and perplexities the grace to ask what thou wouldst have us do, that the spirit of wisdom may save us from false choices, and that in thy light we may see light, and in thy straight path may not stumble; through our Saviour Jesus Christ.

WILLIAM BRIGHT

WHAT WE REALLY NEED   323

O heavenly Father, who knowest our every need: Grant us wisdom to know what things to ask thee for, and grace thankfully to accept and use the powers which thou art ready to bestow; through Jesus Christ our Lord.

Prayers of the Spirit

PRAYER AND THOUGHT   324

Almighty God, who hast bestowed upon us the precious gift of thought, and dost require that we love thee not only with our hearts and souls but also with our minds: Let reason so quicken and give sinew to our prayers, that our devotion, growing mighty with discernment, may shine with wisdom from on high; through Christ our Lord.

JOHN U. STEPHENS

NOT AS I MAY CHOOSE   325

Govern all by thy wisdom, O Lord, so that my soul may always
be serving thee as thou dost will, and not as I may choose. Do
not punish me, I beseech thee, by granting that which I wish
or ask, if it offend thy love, which would always live in me. Let
me die to myself, that so I may serve thee: let me live to thee,
who in thyself art the true Life.

ST. THERESA

(UN)ANSWERED PRAYER   326

He asked for strength that he might achieve; he was made
weak that he might obey.

He asked for health that he might do greater things; he was
given infirmity that he might do better things.

He asked for riches that he might be happy; he was given
poverty that he might be wise.

He asked for power that he might have the praise of men;
he was given weakness that he might feel the need of God.

He asked for all things that he might enjoy life; he was
given life that he might enjoy all things.

He has received nothing that he asked for, all that he
hoped for. His prayer is answered. He is most blessed.

UNKNOWN

FOR SPIRITUAL SIGHT 327

Almighty Father, teach us by thy Spirit how to pray, for indeed
we know not how to pray as we ought. Give us the desire to
speak with thee, and then let us hear thee speak with us. Thy
goodness and loving kindness have followed us day by day. Thy
mercies have been so many that we have dared to deem them
commonplace. Give us the spiritual sight, quick to discern thy
hand and recognize thy bounty. From thee alone come life and
strength, food and raiment, books and friends, work and rest.
Thou givest us these to train us for the better and more abiding
joys. Amid the changes of life, O Lord, keep us steadfast and
loyal to the service of thy will. Let no storm disturb the deep
things of our quietness, no trial shake the foundations of our
faith. Establish us in the assurance that though all else perish,
thy truth and righteousness are eternal; through Christ our
Lord.

SAMUEL MCCOMB

A LAYMAN'S PRAYER 328

Almighty God, we come to seek thy presence here today. Our
hearts have praised thy name in joyful song. Here in thy house
we recall thine ancient mercies. Here is our joy of earth and our
hope of heaven.

We confess unto thee, dear Lord, our many shortcomings
in the week past. As we think back over it we remember how
we have fallen short in thought and word and deed. We have
thought too much about ourselves. We have spoken hastily and
with too little charity. We have labored largely for a greater
share of this world's goods and we have forgotten to seek thy
kingdom and its righteousness first, that all else needful might
be added unto us of thy bounty and care. Forgive us, we pray,
these and all our other faults in thy fatherly love. Take us in
our humility and lift us to a better self in which we may live in

closer company with thee and listen more closely for thy will and word for us.

Dear heavenly Father, we pray this morning for all men. Be with worshipers near and far who call upon thee in varied tongue and song. Look with love upon men of all colors and all honest vocations. Grant thy protection and wisdom to the President of the United States, and all guardians and servants of the public trust. Keep in thy care the men of the armed services, that though they take the wings of the morning and dwell in the uttermost parts of the sea, even there thy hand may lead them and thy right hand may hold them. Look with light and mercy upon any who may live in bondage to sin or in the oppression of any of their neighbors. Speed the day when all the tools of war shall be melted in the triumph of wise men of good will. Let thy kingdom come, and thy will be done, beginning with us here before thee now.

We ask for ourselves that thou give us strength. We ask for strength to earn our daily bread, but ask thee more for the hidden strength which overcomes the world. Touch our lives by thy Spirit, that as workmen in store and office, shop and field, we may do our work for thee. Let us so labor each day that at evening we may offer up our day's work as an adornment of thy earth or as a service to our fellow-men. We ask also for strength to do the right, without wavering, under thy watchful and loving eye. Let us in the power of this moment keep true to its vision of the world that is to be when all life is led in the very fellowship of this hour.

And, lastly, we ask thy peace upon us. Keep our hearts from fretting over the ways of this world. Let us drink here the draughts of silence which set at naught the distractions of the world without. Let thy will for us be our peace, as we resign ourselves to the call of thy word. And may this peace be our sufficient reward as thy children and workmen until the day is done and our spirits rise to rest forever with thee. Be with us and our loved ones all the week long, and hear us when we pray, calling unto thee ever as now in the name of our Lord and Saviour Jesus Christ.

ROBERT L. EDDY

13

Self-Examination

Pray with your intelligence. Bring things to God that you have thought out, and think them out again with Him.

BISHOP BRENT

FORGIVE ME   329

Forgive me my sins, O Lord: the sins of my present and the sins of my past; the sins which I have done to please myself and those done to please others; sins casual and sins deliberate. And forgive the sins which I have so labored to hide that I have hidden them even from myself. Forgive them all, most gracious Lord, for Jesus Christ's sake.

THOMAS WILSON

SORROW AND CONTRITION   330

O Father in heaven, who didst fashion my limbs to serve thee and my soul to follow hard after thee, with sorrow and contrition of heart I acknowledge before thee the faults and failures of the day that is now past. Too long, O Father, have I tried thy patience; too often have I betrayed the sacred trust thou hast given me to keep; yet thou art still willing that I should come to thee in lowliness of heart, as now I do, beseeching thee to drown my transgressions in the sea of thine own infinite love.

My failure to be true even to my own accepted standards:

My self-deception in face of temptation:

My choosing of the worse when I know the better:

O Lord, forgive.

My failure to apply to myself the standards of conduct I demand of others:

My blindness to the suffering of others and my slowness to be taught by my own:

My complacence towards wrongs that do not touch my own case and my over-sensitiveness to those that do:

My slowness to see the good in my fellows and to see the evil in myself:

My hardness of heart towards my neighbors' faults and my readiness to make allowance for my own:

My unwillingness to believe that thou hast called me to a small work and my brother to a greater one:

O Lord, forgive.

JOHN BAILLIE

HE ENTERS WITH COMPASSION 331

I am not sufficient, O Master and Lord, that thou shouldest enter in under the roof of my soul, but since thou in thy love willest to dwell in me I take courage and approach. Thou commandest; I will open wide the doors, which thou alone didst create, that thou mayest enter with compassion as is thy nature; that thou mayest enter, and enlighten my darkened mind. I believe that thou wilt do this, for thou didst not flee away from the sinful woman when with tears she came near to thee, neither rejectedst thou the publican who repented, neither didst thou cast away the thief who confessed thy kingdom, neither didst thou leave the repentant persecutor to himself: but all those who had been brought to thee by repentance, thou didst set in the company of thy friends; O thou who alone are blessed ever, world without end.

ST. JOHN CHRYSOSTOM

STAMPED WITH HIS IMAGE °332

Eternal and most glorious God, who hast stamped the soul of man with thine Image, received it into thy Revenue, and made it a part of thy Treasure: Suffer us not so to undervalue ourselves, nay, so to impoverish thee, as to give away these souls for nothing, and all the world is nothing if the soul must be given for it. Do this, O God, for his sake who knows our natural infirmities, for he had them, and knows the weight of our sins, for he paid a dear price for them; thy Son, our Saviour Jesus Christ.

JOHN DONNE

ASHAMED AND AFRAID 333

O Lord, I have done something wrong and I am afraid I will be found out. I am ashamed, but more than that, I am afraid that people who love me will be ashamed.

O Lord, I know it is my fault that I have done this thing and it cannot be undone, but help me not to be a coward. If I ought to confess to someone, give me the courage. If I can make things better, show me how. And above all, do not let me add bad to bad because I am too afraid to let someone know what I have done.

AVERY BROOKE

THE MERCIES OF OUR FELLOWMEN °334

O Lord, who hast taught us that only as we ourselves forgive can we be forgiven, help us ever to bear in mind our own shortcomings, so that when we remember the injuries we have suffered and never deserved, we may also recall the kindnesses we have received and never earned, and the punishments we have deserved but never suffered; and help us, we pray thee, to give thanks to thee for thy mercies, and for the mercies of our fellowmen; for thy Name's sake.

Prayers Used at Groton School

WHEN WE DESERVE PUNISHMENT 335

Turn thou us, O good Lord, and so shall we be turned. Be favorable, be favorable to thy people, who turn to thee in weeping, fasting, and praying. For thou art a merciful God, full of compassion, long-suffering, and of great pity. Thou sparest when we deserve punishment, and in thy wrath thinkest upon mercy. Spare us then, good Lord, lest we be brought to confusion, and after the multitude of thy mercies look upon us; through the merits and mediation of thy blessed Son, Jesus Christ our Lord.

Book of Common Prayer (USA)

A HUMBLE SPIRIT 336

Give us, O Lord, a humble spirit, that we may never presume upon thy mercy, but live always as those who have have been much forgiven. Make us tender and compassionate toward any who are overtaken by temptation, remembering how we have fallen in times past and may fall yet again. Make us watchful and sober-minded, looking ever unto thee for grace to stand upright, and to persevere unto the end; through thy Son Jesus Christ our Lord.

CHARLES J. VAUGHAN

UNDERSTANDING 337

O God, Father of all, help us to forgive others as we would wish them to forgive us. May we try to understand them as we in turn would like to be understood, in the hope that forgiveness will not be in order. May we see with their eyes, think with their minds, feel with their hearts. Then let us ask ourselves whether we should judge them, or judge ourselves and accept them as children, like us, of one heavenly Father.

WILLIAM BARCLAY

THE DOOR OF OUR SPIRIT 338

Thou who hast taught us of old that only in grace to our brethren can the door of our spirit open to the grace of heaven: Fill us with such a sense of kindred and like need, that we may freely forgive, not out of weakness, but from gratitude for the occasion to make room in our lives for thy love which passeth understanding; for the sake of Jesus Christ our Lord.

UNKNOWN

FORGIVENESS 339

Almighty and everlasting God, from whom and through whom and in whom all things are, from whose hand we, with all the world besides, every moment take our being: We appear before thee humbly to acknowledge that thou art the one true God, boundless in thy power, wisdom, goodness, the maker of all things made, the watchful witness and just judge of all things done.

Have mercy, O Lord, have mercy on us sinners. We repent of our sins, we wish they were undone; they cannot be undone, but thou canst pardon them. We humbly hope to be forgiven.

Help us for thy sake to love our neighbors, all men, wishing them well, not ill; proposing to do them good, not evil; forgiving also all who have offended us, as we by thee hope to be forgiven.

This we ask through the merits of thy Son Jesus Christ our Lord, who liveth and reigneth with thee and the Holy Ghost one God, world without end.

GERARD MANLEY HOPKINS

WHEN THE THUNDER BOOMS   340

Father in Heaven! Reawaken conscience in our breast. Make
us bend the ear of thy spirit to thy voice, so that we may perceive thy will for us in its clear purity as it is in heaven, pure of
our false worldly wisdom, unstifled by the voice of passion.
Keep us vigilant so that we may work for our salvation with fear
and trembling. Oh but grant also that when the Law speaks
most strongly, when its seriousness fills us with dread, when the
thunder booms from Sinai—oh grant that we may hear also a
gentle voice murmuring to us that we are thy children, so that
we will cry with joy, "Abba, Father!"

SØREN KIERKEGAARD

TRUE REPENTANCE   341

O God of truth, who requirest truth in the inward man: Hold
thou thy mirror before our souls, that we may see our sins and
failures for what they really are—neither belittled nor enlarged;
that our repentance may be realistic, and our efforts at reform
intelligent; through him who taught us that only the truth can
set us free, thy Son our Saviour Jesus Christ.

J. W. S.

THAT WE MAY FIND HIM   342

O Lord our God, grant us grace to desire thee with a whole
heart, that so desiring we may find thee, and so finding may love
thee, and loving thee may hate those sins which separate us
from thee; for the sake of Jesus Christ.

ST. ANSELM

HIS VICTORIOUS CONFIDENCE 343

O God, who by the mystery of Christ's uplifted Cross hast drawn men everywhere in penitence unto him, and reconciled them to thee their God: Help us to hate in ourselves those same sins of selfishness and idolatry of power and lust for material things which nailed him, the Sinless One, to the tree—all sins against justice and brotherhood and love. Help us to gain something of his victorious confidence, as he faced death, silent but unafraid, quietly trusting in thy goodness and wisdom. And grant us so to share in his spirit that, united in fellowship with him, and obedient to thy will, we also may through him be partakers in newness of life, even here and now, and in the eternal Easter within thy kingdom. For his Name's sake.

FREDERICK C. GRANT

GRACE TO REFRAIN FROM SIN 344

O God, who knowest the weakness and corruption of our nature, and the manifold temptations which we daily meet with: We humbly beseech thee to have compassion on our infirmities, and to give us the constant assistance of thy Holy Spirit; that we may be effectually restrained from sin, and incited to our duty. Imprint upon our hearts such a dread of thy judgments, and such a grateful sense of thy goodness to us, as may make us both afraid and ashamed to offend thee. And, above all, keep in our minds a lively remembrance of that great day in which we must give a strict account of our thoughts, words, and actions to him whom thou hast appointed the Judge of the living and the dead, thy Son Jesus Christ our Lord.

Book of Common Prayer (USA)

BE STERN WITH US 345

O Spirit of the living God, we pray thee to save us from our evasions and deceits, and the soft complacency with which we excuse ourselves. Let some ennobling word of justice and beauty awaken our conscience. Be stern with us, O living God, and chasten us by strong guidance in righteousness; through him who will come to be our Judge, our Saviour Jesus Christ.

HARRY EMERSON FOSDICK

RENEWAL OF JOY 346

We are evil, O God, and help us to see it and amend. We are good, and help us to be better. Look down upon thy servants with a patient eye, even as thou sendest sun and rain; look down, call up the dry bones, quicken, enliven; recreate in us the soul of service, the spirit of peace; renew in us the sense of joy.

ROBERT LOUIS STEVENSON

CLEARNESS OF SIGHT 347

Touch our eyes, O Lord, with clearness, and place the world before them truly; that we may see through its illusions to its sorrows and sins, and never trust ourselves to it without the shield of faith and the sword of the Spirit, and the unwearied courage of hope and love. Prepare us to seek our rest, not in outward ease, but in inward devotedness; only fulfill unto us the word of the Chief of saints: leave us his peace while we remain here, and then receive us unto thyself, to mingle with the mighty company of our forerunners.

JAMES MARTINEAU

Blessed are the poor in spirit: for theirs is the kingdom of heaven.
Bless us, O God, whensoever we feel poor in spirit; and, by the plenitude of thy grace, enable us to make many rich, as workers together with thee and fellow members of thy kingdom of love; through Jesus Christ our Lord.

Blessed are they that mourn: for they shall be comforted.
Fortify, O Holy Ghost, the spirits of those who mourn; that, consoled by thy gracious compassion, they may be comforted of thee; through him whose promises are faithful, our Saviour Jesus Christ.

Blessed are the meek: for they shall inherit the earth.
Teach us, O God, the courage of gentleness; that, abiding patiently in thee, we may inherit that peace which alone can make the earth our own by making it the home of all thy children; through him who died that all men might live, thy Son Jesus Christ our Lord.

Blessed are they which do hunger and thirst after righteousness: for they shall be filled.
Quicken, O Holy Spirit, the hunger of our hearts for true righteousness; that, pressing toward the mark of our high calling, we may at length be filled with all the fulness of God; through Jesus Christ our Lord.

Blessed are the merciful: for they shall obtain mercy.
Kindle in our hearts, O God, thy compassion, and awaken in us those sympathies which thou didst manifest in thy Son; that, walking in humility and helpfulness with our brothers, we may enjoy the benediction of thy mercy which endureth for ever; through the same, Jesus Christ our Lord.

Blessed are the pure in heart: for they shall see God.
Purify our hearts, we pray thee, O God; that, with clearness of vision and singleness of mind, we may steadfastly look upon the beauty of thy holiness, and follow him in whom it is perfectly revealed; even thy Son, Jesus Christ our Lord.

Blessed are the peacemakers: for they shall be called the children of God.

Make peace in our hearts, we pray thee, O God; that we, building with patience the temple of thy truth among men, may be found worthy to be called thy children, and the friends of thy Son, Jesus Christ our Lord.

Blessed are they which are persecuted for righteousness' sake: for theirs is the kingdom of heaven.

Strengthen, O Lord, our loyalty to every righteous cause; that, when we suffer for our fidelity, we may rejoice to find our place in the citizenship of heaven; where thou reignest, God for ever and ever.

J. W. S.

A PERSONAL LITANY 349

That it may please thee to grant me by thy Holy Spirit to hear ever more clearly thy voice, calling me to a deeper devotion to thy service:

Lord, hear my prayer.

For grace to respond with my whole heart to thy call:

Lord, hear my prayer.

For a continual sense of thine abiding presence and overruling guidance in my daily life:

Lord, hear my prayer.

For a deeper love and earnestness in the act of consecration to thee of myself, my soul and body, that I make anew at each Communion:

Lord, hear my prayer.

For the illuminating grace of thy Holy Spirit, that I may be guided to use for thee every power and every opportunity thou hast given me:

Lord, hear my prayer.

For grace so to live in the light of thy divine love for me that, loving thee above all, I may give to others the sunshine of love which has its source in thee alone:

Lord, hear my prayer.

For spiritual insight to realise more fully my influence on others, and grace to use it only and always for thee:

Lord, hear my prayer.

For wisdom, taught of love, to understand the needs of my friends, and grace to help them by prayer and sympathy:

Lord, hear my prayer.

For a daily renewal of the spirit of true joy which the sense of thine abiding presence alone can give, that all the joys of my life may be sanctified in thee:

Lord, hear my prayer.

For a steadfast heart to meet with constant cheerfulness the anxieties and trials of my life as thy way of sanctification for me:

Lord, hear my prayer.

For inspiration and grace so to worship thee and to serve thee here, that I may be ready for thy perfect service hereafter:

Lord, hear my prayer.

For a right judgment in giving to each duty its due place and proportion, that my days may be ordered in accordance with thy divine will:

Lord, hear my prayer.

For grace to make the spirit in which I fulfil all social duties one with the spirit of my inmost life and prayers:

Lord, hear my prayer.

For grace to refrain from the unkind word, and from the unkind silence:

Lord, hear my prayer.

For guidance so to use the intellectual ability thou hast given that I may continually go forward towards the fulness of that perfection which thou hast purposed for me:

Lord, hear my prayer.

For a spirit of willing self-denial, that I may give gladly and freely for the work of thy Church at home and abroad:

Lord, hear my prayer.

For inward light to see how far short I have come of thy divine purpose for me:

Lord, hear my prayer.

For a truer penitence, a firmer faith, a deeper devotion, a more perfect love:

Lord, hear my prayer.

For a fuller apprehension of thine infinite love for me—of the power of prayer—of the joy of spiritual things—of the glory that shall be revealed:

Lord, hear my prayer.

And grant unto me, unworthy though I am, a clear vision of the beauty of holiness and a sure confidence that in thy light and by thy grace I may at last attain to it; through Jesus Christ my Lord.

W. B. TREVELYAN

A LITANY OF REMEMBRANCE   °350

Seeing, brethren, that we are weak men, but entrusted with a great responsibility, and that we cannot but be liable to hinder the work entrusted to us by our infirmities of body, soul, and spirit, both those common to all and those specially attaching to our work; let us pray God to save us and help us from the weaknesses which beset us severally, that he will make us know what faults we have not known, that he will show us the harm of what we have not cared to control, that he will give us strength and wisdom to do more perfectly the work to which ourselves have been consecrated—for no less service than the honor of God and the edifying of his Church.

O Lord, open thou our minds to see ourselves as thou seest us, or even as others see us and we see others; and from all unwillingness to know our infirmities,

Save us and help us, we humbly beseech thee, O Lord.

O Lord, strengthen our infirmities, especially those which hinder our work beyond our control; give us nerve to overcome the shyness that fetters utterance, and ease for awkwardness of address; turn us from our sensitive consciousness of ourselves, that we may think with freedom of what is in our heart, and of the people with whom we are concerned; and from all hindrances and weakness,

Save us and help us, we humbly beseech thee, O Lord.

From moral weakness of spirit, from timidity, from hesitation, from fear of men and dread of responsibility, strengthen us with courage to speak the truth as our work requires, with a strength that can yet speak in love and self-control; and alike from the weakness of hasty violence and the weakness of moral cowardice,

Save us and help us, we humbly beseech thee, O Lord.

From weakness of judgment, from the indecision that can make no choice, and the irresolution that carries no choice into act, strengthen our eye to see and our will to choose the right; and from losing opportunities and perplexing our people with uncertainties,

Save us and help us, we humbly beseech thee, O Lord.

From infirmity of purpose, from want of earnest care and interest, from the sluggishness of indolence, and the slackness of indifference; and from all spiritual deadness of heart,

Save us and help us, we humbly beseech thee, O Lord.

From dullness of conscience, from feeble sense of duty, from thoughtless disregard of consequences to others, from a low idea of the obligations of our ministry; and from all half-heartedness in our work,

Save us and help us, we humbly beseech thee, O Lord.

From weariness in continuing struggles, from despondency in failure and disappointment, from an overburdened sense of our unworthiness, from morbid fancies of imaginary back-slidings, raise us to a lively hope and trust in thy presence and mercy, and in the power of faith and prayer; and from all exaggerated fears and vexations,

Save us and help us, we humbly beseech thee, O Lord.

From self-conceit and vanity and boasting, from delight in supposed success and superiority, raise us to the modesty and humility of true sense and taste and reality; and from all the harms and hindrances of offensive manners and self-assertion,

Save us and help us, we humbly beseech thee, O Lord.

From affectation and untruth, conscious or unconscious; from acting a part, which is hypocrisy; from impulsive self-adaptation to the moment, to please persons or make circumstances easy, strengthen us to manly simplicity to be, and be seen to be, true men; and from all false appearances,

Save us and help us, we humbly beseech thee, O Lord.

From love of flattery, from overready belief in praise, from dislike of criticism and hatred of independence, and from the comfort of self-deception in persuading ourselves that others think better than the truth of us,

Save us and help us, we humbly beseech thee, O Lord.

From all love of display, and sacrifice to popularity; from thought of ourselves in forgetfulness of thee in our worship, and of our people in our teaching; hold our minds in spiritual reverence, that if we sing we may sing unto the Lord, and if we preach, may preach as of a gift thou givest, not for our glory but for the edification of thy people; and in all our words and works, from all self-glorification,

Save us and help us, we humbly beseech thee, O Lord.

From pride and self-will, from desire to have our own way in all things; from overweening love of our own ideas and blindness to the value of others'; from resentment of opposition, and contempt for the claims of others, enlarge the generosity of our hearts, and enlighten the fairness of our judgments; and from all selfish arbitrariness of temper,

Save us and help us, we humbly beseech thee, O Lord.

From all jealousy, whether of equals or superiors, from begrudging others' success, from impatience of submission and eagerness for authority; give us the spirit of brotherhood to share loyally with fellow-workers in all true proportions; and from all insubordination to law, order, and authority,

Save us and help us, we humbly beseech thee, O Lord.

From all hasty utterances of impatience, from the retort of irritation and the taunt of sarcasm; from all infirmity of temper in provoking or being provoked, from love of unkind gossip; and from all idle words that may hurt,

Save us and help us, we humbly beseech thee, O Lord.

In all times of temptation to leave duty for amusement, to indulge in distraction and dissipation, to degrade our high calling and forget our vows; and in all times of frailty in our flesh,

Save us and help us, we humbly beseech thee, O Lord.

In all times of ignorance and perplexity as to what is right and best to do, direct us with wisdom to judge aright, order our ways and overrule our circumstances as thou canst in thy good Providence; and in our mistakes and misunderstandings,

Save us and help us, we humbly beseech thee, O Lord.

In times of doubts and questionings, when our belief is perplexed by new learning, new teaching, new thought; when our faith is strained by creeds, by doctrines, by mysteries beyond our understanding, give us the faithfulness of learners and the courage of believers in thee; give us boldness to examine and faith to trust all truth; patience and insight to master difficulties; stability to hold fast our tradition with enlightened interpretation, to admit all fresh truth made known to us, and in times of trouble to grasp new knowledge really and to combine it loyally and honestly with the old; and alike from stubborn rejection of new revelations, and from hasty assurance that we are wiser than our fathers,

Save us and help us, we humbly beseech thee, O Lord.

From strife and partisanship and division among the brethren, from magnifying our certainties to condemn all differences, from using our position to promote worldly interest or policy; and from all arrogance in our dealings with men as ministers of God,

Save us and help us, we humbly beseech thee, O Lord.

Give us knowledge of ourselves, our powers and weaknesses, our spirit, our sympathy, our imagination, our truth; teach us by the standard of thy Word, by the judgments of others, by examinations of ourselves; give us earnest desire to strengthen ourselves continually by study, by diligence, by prayer and meditation; and from all fancies, delusions, and prejudices of habit or temper or society,

Save us and help us, we humbly beseech thee, O Lord.

Give us true knowledge of our people, in their differences from us and in their likenesses to us, that we may deal with their real selves, measuring their feelings by our own, but patiently considering their varied lives and thoughts and circumstances; and in all our ministrations to them, from false judgments of our own, from misplaced teaching, from misplaced trust and distrust, from misplaced giving and refusing, and from misplaced praise and rebuke,

Save us and help us, we humbly beseech thee, O Lord.

Chiefly, O Lord, we pray thee to give us knowledge of thee: to see thee in all thy works, always to feel thy presence near, to hear and know thy call. May thy Spirit be our spirit, our words thy words, thy Will our will; that in all our work we may be true prophets of thine; and in all our shortcomings and infirmities may we have sure faith in thee.

Save us and help us, we humbly beseech thee, O Lord.

Finally, O Lord, we humbly beseech thee to blot out our past transgressions, heal the evils of our past negligences and ignorances, and make us amend our past mistakes and misunderstandings. Uplift our hearts to new love, new energy and devotion, that we may be unburdened from the grief and shame of past faithlessness to go forth in thy strength to persevere through success and failure, through good report and evil report, even to the end; and in all time of our tribulation, and in all time of our wealth,

Save us and help us, we humbly beseech thee, O Lord.

O Christ, hear us.
Lord, have mercy upon us.
Christ, have mercy upon us.
Lord, have mercy upon us.

Our Father, who art in heaven, Hallowed be thy Name. Thy kingdom come. Thy will be done, On earth as it is in heaven. Give us this day our daily bread. And forgive us our trespasses, As we forgive those who trespass against us. And lead us not into temptation, But deliver us from evil. Amen.

The grace of our Lord Jesus Christ, and the love of God, and the fellowship of the Holy Ghost, be with us all evermore.

GEORGE RIDDING

14

Inner Peace

Hold thee still in the Lord, and abide patiently upon him.

PSALM 37:7

AT REST FROM OURSELVES 351

O God, let us not seek beyond thee what we can find only in thee: peace and rest, joy and blessedness. Lift our souls above the round of harassing thoughts to the pure bright atmosphere of thy presence, that there we may breathe freely, there be at rest from ourselves and from all things that weary us; and thence return, thy peace within us, to do and bear whatsoever pleaseth thee; through Jesus Christ our Lord.

E. B. PUSEY

WITH A QUIET MIND °352

Grant, we beseech thee, merciful Lord, to thy faithful people pardon and peace, that we may be cleansed from all our sins, and serve thee with a quiet mind; through Jesus Christ our Lord.

Book of Common Prayer (USA)

QUIETNESS 353

O Thou the almighty and eternal One, who hast said, Be still and know that I am God; let our hearts be to thee as quiet waters that even in their little depths can mirror the eternal stars; through Jesus Christ our Lord.

WALTER RUSSELL BOWIE

THE CENTRAL PEACE °354

Almighty God, who art the only source of health and healing, the Spirit of calm, and the central peace of the universe: Grant to us thy children such an awareness of thy presence as may give us utter confidence in thee. In all pain and weariness and anxiety may we throw ourselves upon thy besetting care; that knowing ourselves fenced about by thy loving omnipotence, we may permit thee to give us health and strength and peace; through Jesus Christ our Lord.

CHARLES MORRIS ADDISON

PERFECT PEACE 355

Grant us, O Lord, the blessing of those whose minds are stayed upon thee, that so we may be kept in perfect peace: a peace which cannot be broken. Let not our minds rest upon any creature, but only in the Creator: not upon goods, things, houses, lands, inventions of vanities or foolish fashions, lest, our peace being broken, we become cross and brittle and given over to envy. From all such deliver us, O God, and grant us thy peace.

GEORGE FOX

THE BLESSED BURDEN 356

May the Lord Jesus Christ, whose yoke is easy and whose burden is light, give that rest unto our souls which he promised to all who turn to him, our Master and our Friend.

J. W. S.

LAY HOLD ON GRACE   357

O God, our Creator, who hast given us souls and bodies wonderfully intertwined, and a host of unknown possibilities:
Grant us the wisdom to lay hold on thy grace, that we may
bring order out of confusion, and gain such selfhood as was
achieved by thy Son, Jesus Christ our Lord.

A. E. S.

THE DEEP AND TRANQUIL SPIRIT   °358

We praise thee, O God, for thy power and thy peace; for the
strong pressure of thy will; for the deep and tranquil Spirit
which is thy presence. Each morning we entrust ourselves to
thy faithfulness, each night to thine invincible rest; O Thou
who art more mighty than our needs!

UNKNOWN

QUIET CONFIDENCE   359

O God of peace, who hast taught us that in returning and rest
we shall be saved, in quietness and in confidence shall be our
strength: By the might of thy Spirit lift us, we pray thee, to thy
presence, where we may be still and know that thou art God;
through Jesus Christ our Lord.

Book of Common Prayer (USA)

THE KING IN HIS BEAUTY   360

O God, who on the mount didst reveal to chosen witnesses
thine only-begotten Son wonderfully transfigured, in raiment
white and glistering: Mercifully grant that we, being delivered
from the disquietude of this world, may be permitted to behold
the King in his beauty; who with thee O Father, and thee O
Holy Ghost, liveth and reigneth one God, world without end.

WILLIAM REED HUNTINGTON

OUR BETTER NATURE   361

O God, God of the great open spaces, where beauty and quietness still our souls, where the meaning of life seems obvious
and the problems of life so simple: Quiet the fever in our
minds and the fear in our hearts by the assurance that back of
all the chaos that bewilders us is an Orderliness which can be
achieved; that stronger than all the hatreds which rack humanity
is a Love which will not let us go; that deeper than all the
issues which divide us is the common adventure of our common humanity which unites us; that more compelling to the
real heart of man than the throb of the drums of war, is the
Spirit of our Lord Jesus Christ calling to the angels of our
better nature.

WILLIAM SCARLETT

SERENITY   362

Lord Jesus Christ, serene Son of God, whose will subdued the
troubled waters and laid to rest the fears of men: Let thy majesty master us, thy power of calm control us; that for our fears
we may have faith, and for our disquietude perfect trust in thee;
who dost live and govern all things, world without end.

Prayers of the Spirit

LIKE A STILL LAKE 363

Grant us, O God, grace to surrender ourselves wholly unto thee, keeping our souls still before thee like a still lake; that so the beams of thy grace may be mirrored therein, until our hearts glow with faith and love, and through such stillness and hope we find our strength and gladness in thee, now and for evermore.

JOACHIM EMBDEN

STEADY OUR THOUGHTS 364

Almighty God, we pray thee to steady our thoughts as we contemplate thy strange unyielding love for every man born into the world, knowing that thou wilt keep us in perfect peace if our minds are stayed on thee, our Saviour and Friend.

J. W. S.

DESIGN FOR A MEDITATION 365

Almighty God, unto whom all hearts are open, all desires known, and from whom no secrets are hid—

> God—The Universe—Heaven. We are a part of God. Our hearts are his. He knows them. We could not, even if we would, hide anything from him. Our souls are in his hand.

Cleanse the thoughts of our hearts by the inspiration of thy Holy Spirit—

> If we ask him, God will, in his wisdom, and with his love, take from us our sins, our faults, even the shortcomings that we ourselves are blind to. Our hearts he will sweep with the wind of his infinite power. We shall be cleansed.

That we may perfectly love thee—

> Only with a clean and contrite spirit can we love God. Only then can we stand in his presence.

And worthily magnify thy holy Name—

> The newly cleansed, the pure in heart, can see God. To see him, to stand in his presence, is to worship him.

Through Christ our Lord.

> In Christ, God has given us his likeness. Only in him do we know the face of our Creator. Towards him we look for our strength, our peace.

UNKNOWN

15

Around the Clock

TODAY IS MINE 366

I thank thee, O God, for the day which thou hast made. I will
rejoice and be glad in it. Whether it be bright or dark, I
will accept it without fear or complaint. Whatever it brings,
I will try to meet it as well as I can. And knowing that in
everything thou workest for good with those who love thee, I
will go about my work in quietness and in confidence. Tomorrow I cannot see, but today is mine because it is thine.

THEODORE PARKER FERRIS

THE ENSUING DAY 367

O God, we implore thy grace and protection for the ensuing
day, that we may be just and upright in all our dealings; quiet
and peaceable; full of compassion, and ready to do good to all
men according to our abilities and opportunities. Be graciously
pleased to take us, and all who are dear to us, under thy fatherly
care and protection. These things, and whatsoever else thou
shalt see to be necessary and convenient to us, we humbly beg
through the merits and mediation of thy Son Jesus Christ, our
Lord and Saviour.

Book of Common Prayer (USA)

THE CROWN OF ALL OUR JOYS 368

O Thou in whom we live and move and have our being, who seest where we are blind, who knowest where we are ignorant; do with us this day as thou thinkest best. We ask thee not for earthly blessings, for ourselves or for those we hold most dear, but we pray thee to grant us faith and hope and love without measure. Be thou the crown of all our joys, the abiding shelter in every sorrow, the shepherd of thy flock throughout the world; leading us, through weariness and trouble here, to thy heavenly fold on high, where peace and joy forever dwell, and where thou art all in all; through Jesus Christ our Lord.

JOHN WALLACE SUTER (1859-1942)

THE CENTER OF OUR LIVES 369

O perfect Love, who art the Light of the world: Light thou this day for us, and to this end create and confirm in us the habit of loving kindness in our hearts, and of prayer in our minds; that we may set thee as the sun in the center of our lives, through him who loveth us, our Saviour Jesus Christ.

A. S. T. FISHER

THE DAY RETURNS 370

The day returns and brings us the petty round of irritating concerns and duties. Help us to play the man, help us to perform them with laughter and kind faces, let cheerfulness abound with industry. Give us to go blithely on our business all this day, bring us to our resting beds weary and content and undishonored, and grant us in the end the gift of sleep.

ROBERT LOUIS STEVENSON

THE GIFT OF A NEW DAY   371

We give thee hearty thanks, O Lord, for rest during the past
night, and for the gift of a new day with its many opportunities
of pleasing thee. Grant that we may so pass its hours in the perfect freedom of thy service, that at eventide we may again give
thanks unto thee; through Jesus Christ our Lord.

EASTERN CHURCH DAYBREAK SERVICE

THE NOONTIDE OF GOD'S GRACE   372

Eternal God, who hast neither dawn nor evening, yet sendest us
alternate mercies of the darkness and the day; there is no light
but thine, without, within. As thou liftest the curtain of night
from our abodes, take also the veil from all our hearts. Rise
with thy morning upon our souls: quicken all our labor and our
prayer: and though all else decline, let the noontide of thy
grace and peace remain. May we walk, while it is yet day, in the
steps of him who with fewest hours finished thy divinest work.

JAMES MARTINEAU

A NOON-DAY PRAYER   373

Blessed Saviour, who at this hour didst hang upon the Cross,
stretching forth thy loving arms: Grant that all mankind may
look unto thee and be saved; through thy mercies and merits
who livest and reignest with the Father and the Holy Ghost,
ever one God, world without end.

ARTHUR CLEVELAND COXE

THROUGH THE NIGHT   374

Commune with us, O Lord, at the close of day, and mercifully
abide with us through the night. As with the cooling dew thou
dost refresh the earth, so may the benediction of thy Spirit
bring refreshment to our souls, both this night and all our days;
through Christ our Lord.

JOHN U. STEPHENS

REFRESHING SLEEP   375

We beseech thee, O Lord, to continue thy gracious protection
to us this night. Defend us from all dangers and mischiefs, and
from the fear of them; that we may enjoy such refreshing sleep
as may fit us for the duties of the coming day. And grant us
grace always to live in such a state that we may never be afraid
to die; so that, living and dying, we may be thine; through
Jesus Christ our Lord.

Book of Common Prayer (USA)

THE MIRACLE OF SLEEP   376

Quiet our thoughts, we beseech thee, O Lord, and let thy peace
descend upon our waiting souls; that commending our spirits to
thy holy keeping, we may accept the miracle of sleep; through
Christ our Lord.

Prayers of the Spirit

THE SILENT HOURS 377

Be present, O merciful God, and so protect us through the silent hours of this night, that we who are fatigued by the changes and chances of this fleeting world may rest upon thine eternal changelessness; through Jesus Christ our Lord.

The Grey Book

PERILS OF THE NIGHT 378

Lighten our darkness, we beseech thee O Lord, and by thy great mercy defend us from all perils and dangers of this night; for the love of thy only Son, our Saviour Jesus Christ.

Book of Common Prayer (USA)

MEDITATIONAL FRAGMENTS 379

Dawn
Fling wide, O Lord, the door of this new day. There is sunlight on the path where I must walk with jubilant feet, as becomes one who follows thee.

Midday
What time is it with thee, Lord? Around the sun our earth glides, while millions of other suns dance to the measure of thy mind. Galaxies of worlds expand and contract with thy breathing. As a vesture shalt thou change them and they shall be changed. What time is it with thee, who sittest above the waterflood and inhabitest eternity? Time and Space are thy children, sent to play in the nursery of men's minds.

Nightwatch
They come about me like bees: thoughts of work undone or badly done; regrets and fears and vain futilities. But do thou, good Lord, slip into my brain thine own thoughts one by one, sensible and cool as silver.

Tempo

Quicken my spirit, Lord. Let me not drag my steps as if each one did not bring me nearer to the place which thou hast gone to prepare, or as if one did not wait, the thought of whose welcoming eyes gives life its meaning.

An Answer

Set me free, O Lord, from bitterness and complaining, that I may accept what is: not to leave it as it is, but as a child accepts a problem from his teacher, knowing that there is an answer.

Hush!

Lay thy finger on my mouth. Then shall I be silent, remembering how the morning stars sang together.

Gaiety of Deity

Laugh at me, Lord. Let the medicine of thy mirth heal while it stings. Dispel the humidity of my self-concern. When my thoughts grow tiresome, teach me to laugh with thee until we shatter the tinkling goblets of my emptiness and pride.

UNKNOWN

16

Milestones in the Christian Year

December 16. O SAPIENTIA. O Wisdom, which camest out of the mouth of the Most High, and reachest from one end to another, mightily and sweetly ordering all things: Come and teach us the way of prudence.

December 17. O ADONAI. O Lord of lords and Leader of the house of Israel, who appearedst in the bush to Moses in a flame of fire, and gavest him the Law in Sinai: Come and deliver us with an outstretched arm.

December 18. O RADIX JESSE. O Root of Jesse, which standest for an ensign of the peoples, at whom kings shall shut their mouths, to whom the Gentiles shall seek: Come and deliver us, and tarry not.

December 19. O CLAVIS DAVID. O Key of David, and Sceptre of the house of Israel; that openest and no man shutteth, and shuttest and no man openeth: Come and bring the prisoner out of the prisonhouse, him that sitteth in darkness and the shadow of death.

December 20. O ORIENS. O Day-spring, Brightness of the Light eternal, and Sun of Righteousness: Come and enlighten them that sit in darkness and the shadow of death.

December 22. O REX GENTIUM. O King of the nations, and their Desire; the Cornerstone who makest both one: Come and save man, whom thou formedst of clay.

December 23. O EMMANUEL. O Emmanuel, our King and Law giver, Hope of the nations, and their Saviour: Come and save us, O Lord our God.

Book of Common Prayer
(CHURCH OF THE PROVINCE OF SOUTH AFRICA)

Christmastide

PREPARING FOR CHRISTMAS   381

O blessed Lord Jesus, give us thankful hearts for thee, our choicest gift, our dearest guest.

Let not our souls be busy inns that have no room for thee and thine, but quiet homes of prayer and praise where thou mayst find fit company; where the needful cares of life are wisely ordered and put away, and wide sweet spaces kept for thee; where holy thoughts pass up and down, and fervent longings watch and wait thy coming.

So when thou comest again, O blessed One, mayst thou find all things ready, and thy servants waiting for no new master, but for one long loved and known.

Even so come, Lord Jesus.

A Book of Simple Prayers

OUR CHRISTMAS PLANS   382

Unto Thee, O God, we commit our Christmas plans and hopes; our families and family reunions; our gaieties and our griefs—asking thy blessing upon every thought and endeavor, thy Spirit of charity in our hearts and wisdom in our minds; that when thy Son our Lord cometh he may find us prepared for what he brings, even newness of life; through the same Jesus Christ our Saviour.

Prayers of the Spirit

HEAVENLY RADIANCE   383

O blessed Jesus, Saviour of mankind, at whose birth the night
was filled with heavenly radiance: Lighten the thick darkness
of the world, we pray thee, and dispel the gloom of our miseries
and fears. Have compassion on the peoples of the earth stumbling in confusion, and guide their feet into the way of peace;
for the honor of thy holy Name.

WILLIAM FREDERIC FABER

CHRISTMAS EVE   384

O God, who hast hallowed this sacred night with the joyful
tidings of the Word made flesh: Grant that we, beholding here
on earth as through a veil the mystery of his glory, may at last
see him face to face, in the fulness of thine eternal splendor;
through the same Jesus Christ our Lord.

FREDERICK B. MACNUTT

TOUCHED WITH JOY DIVINE   385

O God of heavenly glory, Source of earthly peace and good
will: May our Christmas be merry because touched with joy
divine; through him who in his purity and love is born in our
hearts today, thy Son Jesus Christ our Lord.

JOHN WALLACE SUTER (1859-1942)

TO KINDLE GLADNESS   386

We praise thee, O God, for the healthful delights of this season: For mirth quickening the blood, uniting us with others
and refreshing us for work; for joy that heightens all our life
and doubles our powers. Help us, we pray thee, to share these
blessings with others, and kindle gladness in their hearts;
through Jesus Christ our Lord.

Services for Broadcasting

FULFILL THE GOOD TIDINGS   387

O gracious Father, who sent not thy Son into the world to condemn the world, but that the world through him might be saved: Fulfil the good tidings of thine angel, and bring great joy to all people, through the Nativity of him who is the Prince of Peace, and to whom, with thee and the Holy Ghost, be glory in the highest now and for evermore.

                                        WILLIAM FREDERIC FABER

PARTAKERS OF THE DIVINE NATURE   388

Almighty God, who didst wonderfully create man in thine own image, and didst yet more wonderfully restore him: Grant, we beseech thee, that as thy Son our Lord Jesus Christ was made in the likeness of men, so we may be made partakers of the divine nature; through the same thy Son, who, with thee and the Holy Ghost, liveth and reigneth one God world without end.

                    Church of England Proposed Book of 1928

CELESTIAL MUSIC   389

O God, to whom glory is sung in the highest, while on earth peace is proclaimed among men of good will: Grant us so to attune our lives to the music of heaven, that we may practise that good will which thou didst send thy Son to reveal to us in the beauty of his most holy life; for the sake of the same our Saviour Jesus Christ.

                                                  J. W. S.

STAR OF HOPE 390

Send, we pray thee O God, into the darkness of our troubled world, the blessed light of thy Son; and may his star of hope so quicken our minds with mercy and truth that we, like the Wise Men of old, may come with exceeding great joy and lay our wisdom and our gifts before him who with thee and the Holy Spirit liveth one God for ever and ever.

Prayers of the Spirit

CHARITY TO ALL 391

O Almighty God, who by the birth of thy holy Child Jesus hast given us a great Light to dawn upon our darkness: Grant we pray thee, that in his light we may see light to the end of our days; and bestow upon us that most excellent Christmas gift of charity to all men, that so the likeness of thy Son may be formed in us, and we may have the ever-brightening hope of everlasting life; through the same Jesus Christ our Lord.

WILLIAM ANGUS KNIGHT

BROADEN OUR HORIZON 392

O God, who hast made the earth for man, and man for thy glory, and who lovest all thy children: Grant that in this time of rejoicing and festivity we may be mindful of our brothers, near and far, who are hungry or cold or lonely, and for whom the star of the Nativity brings no warmth of friendship and no surcease from anxiety or pain. Make us humble and generous, remembering thy blessed Son who warned us against giving only to those from whom in turn we will receive. Broaden the horizon of our kindness, and stir up our wills to a more sensitive and self-denying generosity; that the hearts of all being bound together in mutual helpfulness, the heart of the world may be bound to thee, in whom the whole family in heaven and earth is one. Through Jesus Christ our Lord.

J. W. S.

AFTER CHRISTMAS   393

We thank thee, O Father, for a happy Christmas: for the presents we received, the fun and joy we had, the meals together, the games, the talk.

We thank thee for the peace and goodwill amongst us through the day. Grant that we may take this joy and fellowship with us into all the ordinary days that follow.

Bless all who have been unhappy at Christmastime: those to whom sorrow came, or sickness, and who remember happy times in other years. Bless all who have been forgotten; cheer and comfort them in their loneliness. And help us to share our happiness with others, as Jesus Christ would want us to do.

WILLIAM BARCLAY

The New Year

ANOTHER YEAR   394

O Immortal Lord God, who inhabitest eternity, and hast brought thy servants to the beginning of another year: Pardon, we humbly beseech thee, our transgressions in the past, bless to us this New Year, and graciously abide with us all the days of our life; through Jesus Christ our Lord.

Book of Common Prayer
(ANGLICAN CHURCH OF CANADA)

DAYS THAT ARE GONE   395

Eternal Father, who alone canst control the days that are gone and the deeds that are done: Remove from our memory, we beseech thee, the weight of the past year, that being set free from both the glamor of complacency and the palsy of remorse, we may reach forth unto those things which are before, and press towards the mark for the prize of the high calling of God, in Christ Jesus our Lord.

CHARLES HENRY BRENT

THE OLD YEAR AND THE NEW 396

Almighty Father, as we keep holy time under the deepening shadows of the closing year, we thank thee for all that it hath brought to us of mercy and truth. Receive our sorrow for our sins, and in thine infinite mercy blot them out of the book of thy remembrance. Let not the experiences of the past year be lost upon us. Fix in our minds every lesson of faith and duty which thou hast been teaching us. Take from our hearts the veil that would hide from us the shining of the heavenly light. Before the record of this year has been finished and sealed, grant unto us a fresh consecration, and a deep and honest desire to live according to thy will, as it has been made known to us in Jesus Christ our Lord.

JOHN HUNTER

Lent

UPHELD IN THE HOUR OF TEMPTATION 397

O Lord our God, long-suffering and full of compassion: Be present with us now, we beseech thee, as we come before thee with our sorrows and sins, to ask for thy comfort and forgiveness. We thank thee for this season of thought and prayer, in which we make ready to recall our Saviour's sufferings and to celebrate his triumph. Grant us the aid of thy Holy Spirit, that as we acknowledge our sins and implore thy pardon, we may also be enabled to deny ourselves, and be upheld in the hour of temptation; through Jesus Christ our Lord.

Prayers for the Christian Year
(CHURCH OF SCOTLAND)

THE SNARES WHICH BESET US   398

O God, who didst suffer thine only Son to be tempted, that he might be able to uphold us when we are tempted: Save us, we pray thee, from those snares and temptations which so continually beset us; and so strengthen us by thy good Spirit, that in all things we may be more than conquerors through him who loved us and endured for us the death of the Cross, the same Jesus Christ our Lord.

Prayers for the Christian Year
(CHURCH OF SCOTLAND)

THE WILDERNESS OF TRIAL   399

Almighty God, whose Spirit leads us, as it led thy Son, into the wilderness of trial in order to be tested: Grant that standing in thy strength against the powers of darkness, we may win the victory over all evil suggestions, and with singleness of heart ever serve thee, and thee alone; through him who was in all points tempted as we are, and who therefore has perfect understanding, the same Jesus Christ our Lord.

Prayers of the Spirit

Holy Week

WITH SOLEMN JOY   400

Assist us mercifully with thy help, O Lord God of our salvation, that we may enter with solemn joy upon the meditation of those mighty acts whereby thou hast given us life and immortality; through Jesus Christ our Lord.

Book of Common Prayer (USA)

THE WAY OF THE CROSS   °401

Almighty God, whose most dear Son went not up to joy but first he suffered pain, and entered not into glory before he was crucified: Mercifully grant that we, walking in the way of the Cross, may find it none other than the way of life and peace; through the same thy Son Jesus Christ our Lord.

WILLIAM REED HUNTINGTON

TRIED GOLD   402

Almighty Father, whose Son lifted up against the dark horizon of the world the shining courage of the Cross: Grant that its radiance may kindle in us a fire of devotion that will burn away all cowardice, and leave only the tried gold of constancy and valor; for his sake who having loved his own, loved them unto the end, our Saviour Jesus Christ.

Prayers of the Spirit

IN TIME OF STRESS   403

O God, whose blessed Son did hang upon the shameful Cross, and for our sakes suffered bitter pain: Give to us, we pray thee, the strength to bear our hurts. In fever, let thy peace come upon us; in anguish may thy strength sustain us; and in all pain let our eyes dwell upon thy Son, that we may behold thy goodness and follow thy way in patience and in confidence. More we cannot ask; with less we cannot live.

WILLIAM H. CROUCH

Words from the Cross

Father, forgive them; for they know not what they do.

STRANGE NEW POSSIBILITIES   404

Almighty Father, we thank thee that in Christ thou wast reconciling the world unto thyself, not from outside and stooping down from above, but from within the process of our human life, charging it with strange new possibilities, and opening our eyes to the high calling of God in the same Christ Jesus our Lord.

H. E. W. FOSBROKE

Today shalt thou be with me in paradise.

FRIEND OF SINNERS   405

O God, whose blessed Son said that he had come to seek and to save the lost, and who made himself the friend of sinners: We praise thee that his love went out to meet each one who sought him, as on the Cross he accepted the conversion of one who shared the agony of crucifixion. And grant that we may hasten the day when all will come to the Cross and acknowledge their Lord and Master, Jesus Christ.

H. E. W. FOSBROKE

Woman, behold thy son. Son, behold thy mother.

UNDERSTANDING AND SYMPATHY   406

O Lord Jesus Christ, who on thy Cross didst take loving thought for thy Mother and thy friend: Grant us grace to be always tender and thoughtful with those who are near and dear to us. In our home and in all our friendships, give us, we pray, powers of understanding and sympathy, that through us there may be shed abroad something of thy divinely human love. We ask this in thy Name, and for thy sake.

H. E. W. FOSBROKE

My God, my God, why hast thou forsaken me?

EVEN IN THE DARKNESS   407

Lord Jesus Christ, in the hours of darkness of the soul, when all seems lost, help us, we pray thee, to remember that in thy complete sharing of our human experience there came a time when thou hadst to commit thyself to One, the movement of whose will thou couldst not understand, but must lay thy despairing doubt before a God hidden in the darkness. So give us, we pray, thine unshakeable certainty that even in the darkness God is here; and that even when strangely hidden he declares himself with a power which is available. This we ask for the honor of thy holy Name.

H. E. W. FOSBROKE

I thirst.

SOUNDING THE DEPTHS   408

Lord Jesus Christ, who in thy passion hast sounded the depths of human anguish: Grant, we beseech thee, that in all we are called upon to bear of pain, physical or mental, we may be drawn into deeper sympathy with the pain and grief of others, and into a new sense of union with thy redeeming love. This we ask in thy Name, who with the Father and the Holy Spirit art one God, world without end.

H. E. W. FOSBROKE

It is finished.

THE DIVINE WORK   409

O Christ, who didst finish the divine work thy Father gave thee to do, help us, we beseech thee, to yield ourselves daily to the loving energy of the will of God; to use all the ability he has given us in the making of our plans; to place our planning and our effort in his knowing hands, not prescribing the use he is to make of them, but gladly trusting his wisdom and his love, confident that in union with thee all that is good and true in our striving will be given lasting worth and complete fulfillment; for the honor of thy holy Name.

H. E. W. FOSBROKE

Father, into thy hands I commend my spirit.

HIS VICTORY   410

O Christ, who hast taken the sting from death and robbed the grave of its victory; to whom also is given the Name which is above every name, for thou art Lord of all: We pray that, made children of God through thy victory, and ever strengthened by thy grace, we may continue thine through all our days and in the hour of death; so that by thy mercy we may come to that peace and joy which thou hast prepared for those who love thee; who with the Father and the Holy Spirit art one God for ever and ever.

PAUL ZELLER STRODACH

SOLILOQUY   411

My soul, it is well for thee to gaze on the Cross of thy Redeemer; for when thou dost behold thy Saviour offering himself, mayhap thou wilt be constrained to go and do likewise. Upon that Cross thy Christ offered himself once for all souls, and once for all time. His act of love transcends all countries and all climes; all calendars, all times. It was once upon a time; it is now in all time. It was once on earth; it is now in heaven. So let it be on earth again.

SAMUEL S. DRURY

CONFRONTED BY THE CROSS OF CHRIST   412

O God, we pray thee to confront us with the Cross of Christ, that it may shame us out of self-indulgence and love of luxury, sharpen our consciences to feel involved in every vice or wrong or pain, and render intolerable to us all unjust and needless inequalities. May it give us a new sense of the sacredness of our work, our brethren, and ourselves; may it inspire commerce and industry and legislation with a heart akin to the Son of man's, and lift all education, all science, and all art, to a loftier consecration; and so transform all men, the worst and the best, until all bear the marks of him who died upon the Cross, our Saviour Jesus Christ.

HENRY SLOANE COFFIN

LOVING SERVICE   413

Almighty God, whose only-begotten Son was lifted up from the earth for our salvation: Give us, we pray thee, such a measure of his love and grace, that we may learn to seek only the gain of sacrifice, and strive only for the exaltation of knowing that we serve; that so we may be lifted nearer to him who by his Cross hath redeemed us, the same Jesus Christ our Lord.

J. W. S.

THE VISION OF HIS FACE   °414

Almighty Lord of life, of work and peace, Lord of our wandering wills: Renew, we beseech thee, our souls by the inspiration of thy Holy Spirit, with loyalty to duty and love for it; that when our wills have become one with thine, when our work is judged by thy presence, when this life's turmoil has brought forth its harvest of peace, our souls may see thy face; through his power who liveth and reigneth Lord of death and Source of life eternal, our Saviour Jesus Christ.

FREDERIC PALMER

CHRIST OUR PROTECTOR °415

May the Cross of the Son of God, who is mightier than all the hosts of Satan, and more glorious than all the angels of heaven, abide with you in your going out and your coming in! By day and by night, at morning and at evening, at all times and in all places, may it protect and defend you! From the wrath of evil men, from the assaults of evil spirits, from foes visible and invisible, from the snares of the devil, from all low passions that beguile the soul and body, may it guard, protect, and deliver you.

Book of Common Prayer
(CHURCH OF INDIA, PAKISTAN, BURMA, AND CEYLON)

Eastertide and the Ascension

TRIUMPHANT OVER DEATH 416

O risen and victorious Christ, whose light and love destroyed the darkness of death: Ascend, we pray thee, the throne of our hearts; and so rule our wills by the might of that immortality wherewith thou hast set us free, that we may evermore be alive unto God, through the power of thy glorious resurrection; for the honor of thy holy Name.

Prayers of the Spirit

FROM DESPAIR TO TRIUMPH 417

Almighty and everlasting God, who on Easter Day didst turn the despair of the disciples into triumph by the resurrection of Christ who had been crucified: Give us faith to believe that every good which has seemed to be overcome by evil, and every love which has seemed to be buried in darkness and in death, shall rise again to life immortal; through the same Jesus Christ who liveth with thee for evermore.

WALTER RUSSELL BOWIE

THE PROMISED LAND 418

Eternal God, whose blessed Son by the invincible might of the
Spirit broke the bonds of death and filled heaven with his light:
Enable us by the same Spirit so to lay hold on eternal life, that
we may enter with joy into the promised land where they dwell
who walk in full companionship with thee and thy Son, the
same Jesus Christ our Lord.

J. W. S.

THE LIGHTNING FLASH 419

When thou didst stoop to death, O Life Immortal, and by the
lightning flash of thy divinity didst harrow hell; when from the
lowest parts of earth thou didst raise up the dead; then all the
powers of heaven cried: Giver of life, O Christ our God, Glory
to thee, thou only Lover of mankind.

EASTERN ORTHODOX CHURCH

ASCENSION DAY 420

Who shall speak of thy power, O Lord, or who shall be able to
tell the tale of all thy praises? Thou didst descend to human
things, not leaving behind heavenly things. Thou art returned
to things above, not abandoning things below. Everywhere
thou art thy whole self, everywhere wonderful. Look upon the
prayer of thy people, holy Lord, merciful God; that in this day
of thy holy Ascension, even as glory is given to thee on high, so
grace may be vouchsafed to us below.

Mozarabic Missal

CROWNED WITH GLORY 421

Almighty God, who as at this time raised to thy right hand thy holy Son, and crowned him with everlasting glory: We worship and adore thee in the fellowship of thy redeemed, ascribing to thee and to our Saviour Jesus Christ, in the unity of the Holy Spirit, blessing and honor for ever and ever.

Prayers for the Christian Year

Whitsuntide

WHITSUNDAY 422

O Holy Spirit, who at Pentecost released such power and love that a living faith in Christ spread like fire in the hearts of men: Pour upon us, we pray thee, the same power and love, that we may boldly bear our witness for Christ among men, and by thy grace win their allegiance to him who is the Saviour of the world, the same Jesus Christ our Lord.

THOMAS LEE HAYES

TO GROW UP INTO HIM 423

O God, who on the day of Pentecost didst bring together men from every nation under heaven, to bestow upon them the gift of thy Holy Spirit: Grant unto all who by Baptism are made members of thy Church, that continuing steadfastly in the Apostles' doctrine and fellowship, and in breaking of bread, and in prayers, they may grow up in all things into him who is the head, even Christ our Lord; who liveth and reigneth with thee and the same Spirit ever, one God, world without end.

FRANCIS C. LIGHTBOURN

WORTHY TEMPLES OF HIS PRESENCE °424

O God, who givest thy Holy Spirit without measure to those who prepare for him a dwelling-place: Make us worthy temples of his presence, that, our souls and bodies swept clean of evil, we may joyfully welcome the heavenly Guest in his full splendor, to the sanctification of our lives; through Jesus Christ our Lord, who, with thee and the same Holy Spirit, liveth and reigneth one God forever and ever.

CHARLES HENRY BRENT

17

Affirmations of Faith

AN AFFIRMATION   °425

I believe in God the Father, who has made me and all the
world. I believe in God the Son, who has redeemed me and all
mankind. I believe in God the Holy Spirit, who sanctifies me
and all the people of God. And I believe that my chief end in
life is to glorify God and enjoy him forever.

ADAPTED FROM TWO CATECHISMS

A DECLARATION OF BELIEF   °426

I believe in God, the creator of heaven and of earth, Lord of all
    power and might;
I believe in Jesus Christ, in whom the grace and glory of God
    became incarnate;
I believe in the Holy Spirit by whom the heavenly flame is
    brought to human souls;
I believe in the Oneness of Him who is made manifest in all
    things great and good.
I acknowledge the law of God which is written in the majesty
    of suns and stars;
I acknowledge the truth of God within which alone we can be
    free;
I acknowledge the love of God by which alone we are
    redeemed;

I acknowledge the fellowship of all saints
  Who learned of Christ and lived for Him;
  Who carried in their hearts the flame of consecration and of
    courage,
  Who dared and endured and triumphed even in defeat:
  The evangelists, the apostles, and the martyrs,
  The singers of the triumph of the soul,
  The lovers and the servants of mankind,
  Who gave their lives, and in the giving found all life fulfilled,
  Who in their gentleness were great.
Through them and unto God I lift my soul in thankfulness and
    in eternal praise.

WALTER RUSSELL BOWIE

I BELIEVE   °427

I believe in the dignity of the individual, in government by law,
in respect for the truth, and in a good God. These beliefs are
worth my life, and more.

MCGEORGE BUNDY

FATHER, WORD, SPIRIT   °428

I believe, O Lord, in thee, Father, Word, Spirit: that by thy
natural affection and power the universe has been created; that
by thy love towards mankind the universe has been summed up
in thy Word, who for us men and for our salvation was made
flesh; that by the onshining of thy Holy Spirit we have been
called unto a commonwealth wherein we partake of the communion of saints. And this most holy faith, Lord, I believe;
help thou mine unbelief.

LANCELOT ANDREWES

THE GREATEST HAPPINESS

I believe in God, who is for me spirit, love, the principle of all things.

I believe that God is in me, as I am in him.

I believe that the true welfare of man consists in fulfilling the will of God.

I believe that from the fulfillment of the will of God there can follow nothing but that which is good for me and for all men.

I believe that the will of God is that every man should love his fellow-men, and should act toward others as he desires that they should act toward him.

I believe that the reason of life is for each of us simply to grow in love.

I believe that this growth in love will contribute more than any other force to establish the Kingdom of God on earth: To replace a social life in which division, falsehood, and violence are all-powerful, with a new order in which humanity, truth, and brotherhood will reign.

I believe that the will of God has never been more clearly, more freely expressed than in the teaching of Jesus.

I believe that this teaching will give welfare to all humanity, save men from destruction, and give this world the greatest happiness.

LEO TOLSTOY

GOD'S ETERNAL TRUTH °430

I believe in God, the Almighty Ruler of Nations, our great and good and merciful Maker, our Father in Heaven, who notes the fall of a sparrow, and numbers the hairs of our heads.

I believe in His eternal truth and justice.

I recognize the sublime truth announced in the Holy Scriptures and proven by all history, that those nations only are blest whose God is the Lord.

I believe that it is the duty of nations as well as of men to own their dependence upon the overruling power of God, and to invoke the influence of His Holy Spirit; to confess their sins and transgressions in humble sorrow, yet with assured hope that genuine repentance will lead to mercy and pardon.

I believe that it is meet and right to recognize and confess the presence of the Almighty Father equally in our triumphs, and in those sorrows which, we may justly fear, are a punishment inflicted upon us for our presumptuous sins to the needful end of our reformation.

I believe that the Bible is the best gift which God has ever given to men. All the good from the Saviour of the world is communicated to us through this book.

I believe the will of God prevails. Without Him all human reliance is vain. Without the assistance of that Divine Being, I cannot succeed. With that assistance I cannot fail.

Being a humble instrument in the hands of our Heavenly Father, I desire that all my works and acts may be according to His will; and that it may be so, I give thanks to the Almighty, and seek His aid.

I have a solemn oath registered in heaven to finish the work I am in, in full view of my responsibility to my God, with malice toward none; with charity for all; with firmness in the right as God gives me to see the right. Commending those who love me to His care, as I hope in their prayers they will commend me, I look through the help of God to a joyous meeting with many loved ones gone before.

ABRAHAM LINCOLN

18

The Ageing

O God, our heavenly Father, whose gift is length of days, help us to make the noblest use of mind and body in our advancing years. According to our strength, apportion thou our work. As thou hast pardoned our transgressions, sift the ingatherings of our memory, that evil may grow dim and good may shine forth clearly. Grant us new ties of friendship, new opportunities of service, joy in the growth and happiness of children, sympathy with those who bear the burdens of the world, clear thought and quiet faith. Teach us to bear infirmities with cheerful patience. Keep us from narrow pride in outgrown ways, blind eyes that will not see the good of change, impatient judgments of the methods and experiments of others. Let thy peace rule our spirits through all the trial of our waning powers. Take from us all fear of death, and all despair or undue love of life; that with glad hearts at rest in thee we may await thy will concerning us; through Jesus Christ our Lord.

ISAAC O. RANKIN

FAITH UNSHAKEN 432

Watch over us, O Lord, as our years increase, that we may keep our faith unshaken, our principles immovable. Be thou by our side when the dark hour shall come upon us. May the Cross never grow dim to our eyes, but let its radiance lead us heavenward; and in our hearts may thy peace which passeth understanding abide, all the days of our life.

WILLIAM AMORY GARDNER

TO FIGHT THE GOOD FIGHT °433

Lord God, the Ruler of all things, who fashioned the creation in wisdom, who by thine ineffable forethought and sole will didst bring us to these days: Grant to us, good Lord, to fight the good fight, to finish the course, to keep the faith undivided, and to come without condemnation to thy holy resurrection; for holy is the Name of the Father and the Son and the Holy Spirit, now and ever and for ages of ages.

EASTERN ORTHODOX CHURCH

THE GREEN PASTURES 434

Beneath the light of thy peace may even the valley of the shadow of death be to our feet as the green pastures and the still waters. And when we pass into that land which no eye hath seen, may we be of ready heart to meet our forerunners there, and bless thee that the days of sorrow and temptation are finished.

JAMES MARTINEAU

WITH A QUIET HEART 435

Grant unto us, almighty God, thy peace which passeth understanding; that amid the storms and troubles of life we may rest in thee, knowing that all things are in thee: not beneath thine eye only, but under thy care, governed by thy will, guarded by thy love; so that with a quiet heart we may rejoice to know that darkness and light are both alike to thee. Guide, guard, and govern us even to the end, that none of us may fail to lay hold on the life immortal; through Jesus Christ our Lord.

GEORGE DAWSON

THE GIFT AND THE GIVER 436

Teach me, O Lord, not to hold on to life too tightly. Teach me to hold it lightly; not carelessly, but lightly, easily. Teach me to take it as a gift, to enjoy and to cherish while I have it, and to let go gracefully and thankfully when the time comes. The gift is great, but the Giver is greater still. Thou, O God, art the Giver, and in thee is a Life that never dies.

THEODORE PARKER FERRIS

DEATH WITHOUT FEAR 437

Grant that we here before thee may be set free from the fear of vicissitude and the fear of death, may finish what remains before us of our course without dishonor to ourselves or hurt to others, and, when the day comes, may die in peace.

ROBERT LOUIS STEVENSON

LIFE'S EVENING 438

Lord Jesus Christ, who didst abide with thy two disciples when it was toward evening and the day far spent: Tarry with us, we pray thee, in the evening of life, and make thyself known to us anew as we approach the valley of the shadow, assuring us by thy mercy that thou wilt stay with us to the end.

J. W. S.

GOD'S GLORIOUS MORNING 439

O Thou, whose years are throughout all generations, and who abidest though all else passes away; we pray for those whose days are far spent. Amid the shadows of evening grant them the vision of thy glorious morning. Teach them to bear with patience the infirmities of age. Comfort and sustain them with the hands of friendship and love and sympathy. In loneliness be thou to them their faithful Companion, the same yesterday, today, and forever. Take from them all despair of the world; all regret of vanished days; all impatience with the plans and interests of the present. Give them a forward look, a joyous faith; and when life's day is ended, grant them to rest in the assurance that thou hast in store for them such good things as pass man's understanding. Hear this our prayer for the sake of our Saviour Jesus Christ.

SAMUEL MCCOMB

SOLILOQUY IN THE EVENING OF LIFE °440

My soul, thou canst be thankful for all the mysteries, the greatest of which is death. Thou hast feared the great transition, thou hast clutched at familiar scenes and feared to launch away. Yet thy death shall be a birth elsewhere, and thy transition the entrance to freer realms. Fill every day with deepest living, O my soul. Thus thy time shall be no hurry-scurry nor fearing of the dark, but a smiling pilgrimage lit by Christ and fed by him. Then when the end cometh, wave to this fair realm a brave good-by, and without repining trust the larger hope.

SAMUEL S. DRURY

THE NIGHT ALSO IS THINE 441

Lord, this day has been one glad song, for thou hast been my near companion, pouring thy friendship into my soul. Thou, the arbiter of the world which thou hast made, art the lover of such a least child as I. Make many, O Lord, the hours when I am conscious of thy ministering love. Reveal thyself to me in the joys and pleasures of life, that I may use them for thee and with thee. Summer fades, the summer of life; and winter comes, the winter of death. If I have learned to know thee in the day, I cannot fail, when night falls, to know that the night also is thine.

CHARLES HENRY BRENT

THY LIGHT IN DARKNESS °442

Abide with us, O most blessed and merciful Saviour, for it is toward evening and the day is far spent. As long as thou art present with us, we are in the light. When thou art present, all is brightness, all is sweetness. We discourse with thee, live with thee and lie down with thee. Abide then with us, O thou whom our soul loveth; thou Sun of righteousness with healing under thy wings, arise in our hearts. Make thy light then to shine in darkness, as a perfect day in the dead of night.

HENRY VAUGHAN

19

Sickness and Health

*Joy and pain are complementary. We must enjoy life to
realize its value, but we must suffer to understand its meaning.
There is something beyond joy and pain, including both,
transcending both.*

UNKNOWN

TOTAL HEALING   443

Almighty God, who didst inspire thy servant Saint Luke the
Physician to set forth in the Gospel the love and healing power
of thy Son: Manifest in thy Church the like power and love,
to the healing of our bodies and our souls; through the same
Jesus Christ our Lord.

CHARLES MORRIS ADDISON

TO ACCEPT GOD'S HEALING   444

O God, the source of all health: So fill our hearts with faith in
thy love, that with calm expectancy we may make room for thy
power to possess us, and gratefully accept thy healing; through
Christ our Lord.

Prayers of the Spirit

BEFORE AN OPERATION 445

Strengthen me, I beseech thee O God, to do what I have to do, and bear what I have to bear; that accepting thy healing gifts in the skill and patience of doctors and nurses, I may be restored to usefulness in thy world with a thankful heart; through Christ our Lord.

ROBERT N. RODENMAYER

FOR SLEEP AND REST °446

Eternal and everlasting God,
In the growing quietness of the evening and the deepening
    shadows of the night,
Grant us sleep and rest.
With the stilling of the day's doings, and the end of coming
    and going about us,
Make us to be sleepy with heavy eyes and tired limbs.
As thy creatures are lying down in the wood,
As the bird is quiet in its nest
And the wild thing in its hole,
As the stream is still in its bed
Reflecting the great expanse of stars above,
May we in our sleep reflect our confidence in thee,
And our assurance in thy constant peace.
In our sleep give us that deeper communion of our souls
With thee, which restoreth unto health. For thy Name's sake.

RUSSELL L. DICKS

CONVALESCENCE   447

When I begin to feel better, Lord, let me not forget thee. If I turn to thee when I am in trouble, how much more shall I turn to thee when I am not in trouble:

To thank thee for all my health, and for the prospect of brighter days ahead.

To ask thee for the good sense to enjoy my health, but not to waste it.

To offer thee my body, my will, my mind.

THEODORE PARKER FERRIS

FOR A SICK CHILD   448

Almighty and merciful God, giver of all power and peace: Watch thou with us, we pray thee, over this thy child. Walk with him through the valley of sickness, and lead him forth beside the waters of comfort, where, trusting in thy loving-kindness, he may be made well again; through Jesus Christ our Lord.

Prayers of the Spirit

IN THE PRESENCE OF A SICK CHILD   °449

O Loving Father, we thank you for watching over this child with us, and staying with him day and night. Please help him to get well and strong again as soon as possible; through Jesus Christ our Lord.

J. W. S.

ANOTHER DAY   450

This is another day, O Lord. I know not what it will bring
forth, but make me ready, Lord, for whatever it may be. If I
am to stand up, help me to stand bravely. If I am to sit still,
help me to sit quietly. If I am to lie low, help me to do it
patiently. And if I am to do nothing, let me do it gallantly.
Make these words more than words, and give me the Spirit of
Jesus.

THEODORE PARKER FERRIS

HIDDEN BLESSING   451

O God, if thou shouldst call us to bear pain or sorrow, give us
patience that we may win from it a hidden blessing. And to
this end grant that we may not speak too much about our
griefs, nor let them prey upon our hearts, but commit them all
to thee, casting all our care upon thee because thou carest for
us

SAMUEL MCCOMB

A STOUT HEART   452

O Lord our God, who dwellest in pure and blessed serenity
beyond the reach of mortal pain, yet lookest down in unspeakable love and tenderness upon the sorrows of earth: Give us
grace, we beseech thee, to understand the meaning of such
afflictions and disappointments as we are called upon to
endure. Deliver us from all fretfulness. Give us a stout heart
to bear our own burdens, a willing heart to bear the burdens of
others, and a believing heart to cast all burdens upon thee.
Glory be to thee O Father, and to thee O Christ, and to thee
O Holy Spirit, for ever and ever.

JOHN BAILLIE

THE LONG ROAD 453

O God, who through thy Son hast taught us that thou knowest what is in man: Help us to understand ourselves. When we walk the road of pain, and the miles stretch out ahead and we long for rest, teach us to rely upon thy strength. Accept our faith, feeble as it may seem to us, for it is all we have. And help us to know that however deep the darkness now, we shall by thy mercy come with thankful hearts to the safe lodging of thy peace; through Jesus Christ our Lord.

Prayers of the Spirit

RESTLESSNESS 454

O God, I am weary with restlessness.
Make me to be still.
Make me to be at peace in my soul,
And my muscles to give over their tension.
Make me to know that as I rest upon my bed,
So I rest in thee and in thy support.
In thy peace I would abide all the days of my life,
In thy house would I lie down unto deep slumber.

RUSSELL L. DICKS

FOR ONE NEEDING SLEEP 455

O heavenly Father, who givest thy children sleep for the refreshing of their souls and bodies: Grant this gift to thy servant; keep him in that perfect peace which thou hast promised to those whose minds are stayed on thee; and inspire him with a sense of thy presence, so that in the hours of silence he may enjoy the blessed assurance of thy love; through Jesus Christ our Saviour.

Book of Common Prayer
(CHURCH OF IRELAND)

THE DISQUIETED   456

Regard, O Lord, with thy fatherly compassion, all who are disquieted and tense, who cannot lose themselves either in happy
work by day or in restful sleep by night; who looking within do
not know themselves, and looking to thee do not find thee.
Graciously lead them out of despair into the sure serenity of
truth, out of futility into usefulness, out of confusion into
quiet confidence. Help them to believe that all the darkness
of the world, even the inner blackness of the soul, cannot
quench one small candle of fidelity. Be so patient with them
that they may learn to be patient with themselves, and by
thy mercy venture out and find pasture in sunny fields where all
who follow thy shepherding restore their souls in gladness;
through him who is the world's true Light, our Saviour Jesus
Christ.

Prayers of the Spirit

MENTAL ILLNESS   °457

Almighty and merciful God, we lift up our hearts to thee for
all who are the prey of anxious fears, who cannot get their
minds off themselves, and to whom every demand brings the
feeling that they cannot cope with what is required of them.
Give them the comfort of knowing that this is illness, not cowardice; that millions have felt as they feel; that there is a way
through this dark valley, and light at the end of it. Lead them
to those who can show them the pathway to health and happiness. Sustain them by the knowledge that the Saviour knows
and understands all our woe and fear; and give them enough
courage to face each day, and to rest their minds in the thought
that thou wilt see them through.

LESLIE D. WEATHERHEAD

FOR NURSES   458

Almighty God, in whom wisdom and strength and compassion
are so wonderfully blended, we ask thy blessing upon the nurses
in hospitals or homes who tend the sick, and upon all who are
appointed to assist them. Teach them when to console and
when to challenge. May they temper sympathy with wisdom
and insight. In every person committed to their care may they
see the image of the Creator. When they are tired, refresh
them by thy Spirit; in darkness be thou their Light; in times of
stress, give them quiet courage. And bestow upon them all,
we beseech thee, a share of that imagination and sensitiveness
which beautified the ministry of thy blessed Son, our Saviour
Jesus Christ.

Prayers of the Spirit

20

For the Dying

IN THE HOUR OF TRIAL °459

O God of mercy, suffer us not for any pains of death to fall from thee. From thee indeed we cannot fall, but from our knowledge of thy presence. May we not have any unrighteous thought of thee, or any less worthy than we had in the sweetest hours of communion when all was well; but let us stand upright at thy door, O Lord and lover of souls, looking for the face long desired, the face of uttermost Love.

Through Prayer to Peace

REFRESHED BY HIS GRACE °460

Almighty God, who didst send thy Son from heaven to be Bread of the world and Wine of the soul: Grant that our spirits may be so refreshed by his grace, that we may walk without fear in the highway of eternal life; through the same Jesus Christ our Lord.

J. W. S.

IN QUIET ASSURANCE   461

Immortal Father, from whom we come and to whom we
return, hear our prayer for this thy servant (. . .). Strengthen
and comfort *him* with a sense of thy peace. Grant *him* so to
place his trust in thee, that though *he* walk through the valley
of the shadow of death *he* will fear no evil. May *he* put *his*
hand in thine, and in quiet assurance pass with thee, as a child
with *his* father, to thy home of love and joy and rest, where all
may meet at last in thy many mansions above; through Jesus
Christ, our blessed Lord and Saviour.

SAMUEL MCCOMB

INTO THY HANDS   462

Into thy hands, almighty Father, we commend the soul of this
thy servant (. . . .), as into the hands of a faithful Creator
and most merciful Saviour, in whose sight it is precious; in the
Name of him who will come to be our Judge, and who alone
has perfect understanding, Jesus Christ our Lord.

ADAPTED FROM *Book of Common Prayer* (USA)
AND *Book of Common Prayer*
(CHURCH OF SOUTH AFRICA)

21

For the Departed and the Bereaved

Thou also shalt light my candle; the Lord my God shall make my darkness to be light.

WHERE LIGHT ABOUNDS   463
AND LIFE REIGNS

O King of Paradise, where light abounds and light reigns: Give to our dear ones who are with thee a full share of thy treasures, that they may always be white with thy purity, tranquil with thy peace, and glad with thy joy. Let us live vividly in their present love as they live in ours, until we are taken to the place whither they have gone before, there to dwell in the perfect fellowship that knows no end; for the honor of thy holy Name.

CHARLES HENRY BRENT

POWERFUL AND TENDER TIES   464

Lord of heaven and of earth, we pray thee for all thy servants who have entered into the victory of eternal life, whose living was light to our darkness, and whose death, revealing their immortal stature, binds us with powerful and tender ties to heaven and to thee; through Jesus Christ our Lord.

SAMUEL H. MILLER

INTO HIS PRESENCE   465

O God, whose love embraces thy whole family in heaven and earth: Grant that this thy servant, whom we love but see no longer, having laid aside the garment of mortality may enter more and more into thy presence, and find therein the fullness of joy; through Jesus Christ our Lord.

Prayers of the Spirit

HAPPY MEMORIES   466

O God of all the living, we thank thee for the happy memory of those whom thou hast called out of this transitory life into the eternal joy of thy presence. Thine they were upon the earth, as we are thine; and thine they are still, though our eyes cannot see them nor our ears hear their remembered voices. We thank thee for their lives of loyal service, for the days we spent in their companionship, the example of their faith and courage and patience, and the teaching of their words and deeds. To thee we confess our neglects and transgressions which we may no more confess to them. Our hearts are at rest, knowing that thy love never changes and that they see thy face with unobstructed vision; beseeching thee to give us grace so to live that they may welcome us with joy when at last thou shalt call us to thyself, who holdest all souls in life now and for evermore.

Offices for Special Occasions

A GOOD LIFE WELL LIVED   467

We thank thee, O God, for all the goodness and courage which have passed from the life of this thy servant into the lives of others, leaving the world fairer than it was: for a life's task faithfully and honorably discharged, for gracious and kindly generosity, for sadness met without surrender and weakness endured without defeat. Glory be to thee, O Lord Most High.

UNKNOWN

ABOVE OUR DARKNESS 468

Eternal God, our heavenly Father, who lovest us with an ever-lasting love, and canst turn the shadow of death into the morning: Help us now to wait upon thee with reverent and submissive hearts. In the silence of this hour speak to us of eternal things, that through patience and comfort of the scriptures we may have hope, and be lifted above our darkness and distress into the light and peace of thy presence; through Jesus Christ our Lord.

Book of Common Order
(CHURCH OF SCOTLAND)

IN PARADISE AND ON EARTH 469

O Eternal Lord God, who holdest all souls in life: Vouchsafe, we beseech thee, to thy whole Church in paradise and on earth, thy light and thy peace; and grant that we, following the good examples of those who have served thee here and are now at rest, may at the last enter with them into thine unending joy; through Jesus Christ our Lord.

Book of Common Prayer (USA)

IN THANKFUL REMEMBRANCE 470

Grant, O Lord, to all who are bereaved, the spirit of faith and courage, that they may have strength to meet the days to come with steadfastness and patience; not sorrowing as those without hope, but in thankful remembrance of thy great goodness in past years, and in the sure expectation of a joyful reunion in the heavenly places; and this we ask in the Name of Jesus Christ our Lord.

(CHURCH OF IRELAND)
Book of Common Prayer

A SENSE OF NEARNESS 471

O Christ, who sustained us upon the mountain peak, walk with us now. Quicken within us a sense of thy nearness, that in thee our loved one may draw near and walk with us along a road no longer dark and lonely, but alight with hope and love.

GRACE CARPENTER

OUR LOVE AND SORROW 472

Help us, O Lord, to know that as we give our loved one into thy hands, we give also into thy heart all our love and sorrow, and our penitence for whatever more we might have done in this earthly life. We pray thee to forgive us as we have forgiven each other; to keep alive and true in us our mutual love; and finally to bring us face to face with thy glory, thy loving presence among us all, according to the promise of thy blessed Son, our Saviour Jesus Christ.

UNKNOWN

ACQUAINTED WITH GRIEF 473

O Man of sorrows, and acquainted with grief, who knowest the depth of human pain, grant us grace to read our tragedies in the context of eternal love. Help us to know, even when we cannot understand, that in all things the Father worketh for good with those who love him; and teach us to do our part. Help us to realize that though the price of human love is the risk of loss, only through the love of those we have seen may we understand how to love him whom we have not seen. Grant that through our sorrow we may see more deeply into the hearts of all who suffer; and strengthen our hands to help. Finally, O Lord, open our eyes to behold the reality of the world unseen, where live the blessed dead in thy companionship.

CHARLES T. WEBB

MEDITATION IN SORROW   474

O God, the author of all true and tender affections: Behold
our grief, whose depth is the measure of a love which was thy
gift. Out of the deep we call upon thy Name, for there is
mercy with thee, and in thy Word is our trust. Save us, O
Father, even while the waves of sorrow engulf us. Help us to
entrust to thine eternal keeping the deathless love which binds
us to one whose going from our sight makes our heart faint
within us. Steady us to hold with tranquil hand the candle of
faith, a flame undying amid the changes and chances of our
mortality. So shall we permit thee to guide our steps along the
hard path which lies before us, and which, if we are true, will
reveal itself as the highway of the King who reigneth over heav-
en and earth, our Saviour Jesus Christ.

Prayers of the Spirit

THE WONDERFUL GRACE AND VIRTUE   °475

Almighty and everliving God, we yield unto thee most high
praise and hearty thanks for the wonderful grace and virtue
declared in all thy saints, who have been the choice vessels of
thy grace, and the lights of the world, in their several generations; most humbly beseeching thee to give us grace so to follow the example of their steadfastness in thy faith, and obedience to thy holy commandments, that at the day of the general
Resurrection we, with all those who are of the mystical body of
thy Son, may be set on his right hand and hear that his most
joyful voice: Come, ye blessed of my Father, inherit the kingdom prepared for you from the foundation of the world.
Grant this, O Father, for the sake of the same thy Son Jesus
Christ, our only Mediator and Advocate.

Book of Common Prayer (usa)

22

Benedictions

476

Now to the Holy Spirit that sanctifies us, with the Father that made and created us, and the Son that redeemed us, be given all honor and glory, world without end.

THOMAS CRANMER

477

To the Lord our God, who hath made the heaven and the earth by his great power and by his outstretched arm; to the King of kings and Lord of lords, who only hath the gift of immortality, dwelling in the light which no man can approach unto; to the high and holy One that inhabiteth eternity; be ascribed all might, majesty, dominion and power, henceforth and for evermore.

A. S. T. FISHER

478

Go forth into the world in peace; be of good courage; fight the good fight of faith; that you may finish your course with joy. And the blessing of God Almighty, the Father, the Son, and the Holy Ghost, be upon us, and remain with us for ever.

Book of Common Prayer
(CHURCH OF THE PROVINCE OF SOUTH AFRICA)

479

Under the canopy of the triune God, Blessed Father, Beloved Son, and Gracious Spirit, walk into the future with faith and hope and love. And to him who alone is able to keep us from falling, the Shepherd of our souls and Captain of our salvation, we entrust ourselves, our loved ones, and all for whom we pray, both now and for evermore.

A. NORMAN ROWLAND

480

The grace of God the Father and the peace of our Lord Jesus Christ, through the fellowship of the Holy Spirit, dwell with us forever.

JOHN CALVIN

481

Unto God's gracious mercy and protection we commit this (town) (city): all who abide here; all who bear the authority of government and administration. The Lord bless and keep us all: the prosperous and the impoverished, the neglected, the prisoners, the handicapped, the unemployed; the very old and the very young. The Lord increase in us a sense of community. May he strengthen in us the certainty that we are members one of another, and that if one member suffer, all the members suffer with him. And may the peace and strength and beauty of God abide in our hearts, to steady our minds and quicken our wills to do his Will, now and ever.

WILLIAM SCARLETT

482

May God, the Lord, bless us with all heavenly benediction, and make us pure and holy in his sight. May the riches of his glory abound in us. May he instruct us with the word of truth, inform us with the Gospel of salvation, and enrich us with his love; through Jesus Christ our Lord.

Gelasian Sacramentary

483

The eternal and ever-blessed Father, source of all Light and Life, so fill us with his grace and heavenly benediction, that Christ, who is the brightness of his glory, may dwell in us and we in him, both now and evermore.

A Book of Collects

484

May the blessing of God Almighty, the Father, the Son, and the Holy Spirit, rest upon us, and upon all our work and worship done in his Name. May he give light to guide us, courage to support us, and love to unite us, now and forever more.

UNKNOWN

485

May the Father of all mercies, and God of all comfort, support us in all our tribulations; that we may be able to strengthen those who are in any trouble, by the grace wherewith we ourselves are comforted of God.

UNKNOWN

486

Now God himself and our Father and our Lord Jesus Christ make us to increase and abound in love one toward another, and toward all men; that he may establish our hearts unblameable in holiness before him.

UNKNOWN

487

The Lord hear us and bless us: May he deliver us from our spiritual enemy, and from all that is evil, and keep us under the shadow of his wings, this day and forever.

UNKNOWN

488

Let us wait upon the Lord, for he will renew our strength; so shall we mount up with wings as eagles, run and not be weary, walk and not faint, knowing that in everything God works for good with those who love him; to whom be all thanks, praise, dominion and glory, world without end.

ISAIAH 40:31 AND ROMANS 8:28

489

Grace be unto us, and peace, from God our Father, and from the Lord Jesus Christ, in whom we have redemption and the forgiveness of our sins; to whom be all honor and glory now and forever.

PHILIPPIANS 1:2 AND EPHESIANS 1:7

490

The God of all love, who is the source of our affection for each
other, take our friendships into his own keeping; that they may
continue and increase throughout life and beyond it.

WILLIAM TEMPLE

491

May the grace of the Lord Jesus sanctify us and keep us from
all evil; may he drive far from us all hurtful things, and purify
both our souls and bodies; may he bind us to himself by the
bond of love, and may his peace abound in our hearts now and
for evermore.

Gregorian Sacramentary

492

The Lord enrich us with his grace, and further us with his
heavenly blessing; the Lord defend us in adversity and keep us
from all evil; the Lord receive our prayers, and graciously absolve
us from our offences.

Gregorian Sacramentary

493

May God the almighty direct our days in his peace, and grant
us the gifts of his blessing; may he deliver us in all our troubles,
and establish our minds in the tranquillity of his peace; and may
he so guide us through things temporal that we finally lose not
the things eternal.

Gregorian Sacramentary

494

God the Father, maker of men; God the Son, born amongst men; God the Holy Spirit, sanctifying men: Bless, preserve and keep us, and all whom we love, and all who need our prayers, now and for evermore.

R. AMBROSE REEVES

495

May the strong deliverer and loving Father deliver us from all unworthy fears; the immortal light of Wisdom deliver us from wilful ignorance; and the mighty Spirit so bless us with sincerity in mind and heart and will, that we may ever enjoy the power of Christ, and rest in his peace.

Services for Broadcasting

496

Eternal Light, shine in our hearts;
Eternal Goodness, deliver us from evil;
Eternal Power, be our support;
Eternal Wisdom, scatter the darkness of our ignorance;
Eternal Pity, have mercy upon us;
 through Jesus Christ our Lord.

ALCUIN

497

May the almighty God give us grace
 Not only to admire but to obey his doctrine;
 Not only to profess but to practise our faith in him;
 Not only to love but to live his gospel:
 That what we learn of him we may receive into our hearts,
 And show forth in our lives,
 Through the might of Jesus Christ our Lord.

UNKNOWN

498

God the Father, God the Son, God the Holy Spirit, bless, preserve, and keep us. The Lord mercifully with his favor look upon us, and fill us with all spiritual benediction and grace; granting us in this world knowledge of his truth, and in the world to come life everlasting.

Book of Common Prayer (USA)

499

May God bless us with a loving sense of his near presence, to guide us, to protect us, to help us; that we may know what it is to walk close with him all our life long.

UNKNOWN

500

May the grace of courage, gaiety, and the quiet mind, with all such blessedness as belongeth to the children of our heavenly Father, be ours this day; to the praise and glory of his holy Name for evermore.

UNKNOWN

501

May the King eternal, immortal, invisible, the only wise God, bless and protect us, this day and forever.

I TIMOTHY 1:17

502

Now unto him who is able to keep us from falling, and to present us faultless before the presence of his glory with exceeding joy: to God our Saviour be all majesty, dominion, and power, for ever and ever.

JUDE: 24, 25

503

The Lord bless us and keep us. The Spirit of the Lord cleanse and purify our inmost hearts, and enable us to shun all evil. The Lord enlighten our understandings and cause the Light of his Truth to shine into our hearts. The Lord fill us with faith and love towards him. The Lord be with us day and night, in our coming in and going out, in our sorrow and in our joy, and bring us at length into his eternal rest.

UNKNOWN

Notes

1. The late Dr. Baillie's prayers, beautifully expressed, penetrate deeply into the frailties of our human nature.

3. Thomas Merton, a Trappist Monk, poet, and essayist, is the author of *The Seven Storey Mountain*.

7. From a holograph which shows Bishop Brent's first draft and its revision. His style was markedly individual, as shown in his fondness for colorful metaphors.

13. Adding the words *vesture of* helps the worshipper who does not have the book before him, and therefore might think that "fold in a single *peace*" meant "fold in a single *piece*".

37. In *A Short History of the Book of Common Prayer*, Dr. William Reed Huntington, who led the revision of 1892, named as authors of this prayer "Winthrop and Locke," the latter rector for 52 years of St. Michael's in Bristol, R.I. The prayer was admitted to the Prayer Book in 1928, but with some of its finest phrases either omitted or watered down. The present version follows the original more closely.

43. Eloquent teacher and preacher, and a lover of poetry, Dr. Coffin's style as a writer of prayers matched his skill in composing and conducting liturgical worship: rhythmic, fluent, and sustained.

46. The author, who wrote this prayer for the League of Women Voters, adds, "The time has certainly passed when we could ask God to give us good government without seeing ourselves as His instruments to achieve it."

57. George Zabriskie, a lawyer, and an active member of the Commission to propose the revision of the American Prayer Book (1928), wrote also the prayer For a State Legislature, and the one For Courts of Justice.

59. Archbishop Laud's friendship with Charles I, his refusal to follow extreme reformers, and his use of his official powers, led to his execution by the High Court of Parliament, on whose behalf he had written what is substantially this eloquent prayer.

62. From Epistle 30, "To A Suffering Friend" (1653). Originally in the second-person singular, it is here re-phrased in the first-person plural.

67. The first Prayer Book in the English language (1549) was made by a group of scholars who understood Latin. Usually their translations were faithful to the original. This prayer is an exception. In Latin it reads: "that we may so pass through temporal good things, that we lose not those that are eternal." By deleting the word *good* before *things*, the translators

changed the intent of the petition, which had been to ask for guidance in our use of the good things of our earthly life. The present version restores the original purpose.

69. Parts of many prayers, and quotations from the Bible, are built into this litany, whose only originality is its arrangement.

78. Rev. Robert Noel Rodenmayer, author and editor, was Professor of Pastoral Theology at the Church Divinity School of the Pacific, 1952-1962.

82. In 1861 in Oxford, England, William Bright's *Ancient Collects* made its first appearance. The main body of this remarkable book consists of learned translations of prayers, most of them from the ancient Sacramentaries, including several from the Eastern Liturgies. A 37-page Appendix on the Collects in the Prayer Book follows. Dr. Bright then added 19 collects of his own, in imitation, as he put it, of the ancient model. Included here are numbers 81, 82, 95, 99, 123, 136, 317, 322.

83. Dr. A. S. T. Fisher, late Abbot Scholar at Christ Church, Oxford, published *An Anthology of Prayers* in 1934. Not the least of its merits is the inclusion of prayers from his own pen, of which this is an example.

87. Thanks to the untiring efforts of Raoul Follereau, 116 nations annually observe World Leprosy Day. The Leprosy Relief Society raises funds to provide up-to-date medical treatment. Follereau writes that even in the 20th century he has seen lepers "in prisons, shut up with the insane, locked in an unused cemetery, and in a desert surrounded with barbed wire and machine-guns."

91. Dr. Reinhold Niebuhr, as one of his admirers puts it, makes the unique attempt to relate genuine Christianity to the contemporary world by taking both with equal seriousness.

96. Among contemporary writers who venture to publish prayers exclusively of their own authorship, John Underwood Stephens occupies a place of high distinction.

100. Bishop Charles Francis Hall wrote this prayer for the Service of Thanksgiving to mark the 150th Anniversary of the Diocese of New Hampshire, in 1952.

101. *Prayer Book Studies XVI*, 1963, a revision of two earlier Studies, combines the Calendar with The Collects, Epistles, and Gospels for the Lesser Feasts and Fasts, proposed for future use in the Episcopal Church. It is published by the Church Pension Fund, for the Standing Liturgical Commission. Three of the proposed collects honor respectively, John Chrysostom, Bishop of Constantinople; Thomas Aquinas, Friar; and Gregory the Great, Bishop of Rome. See also prayers 134 and 145.

104. This prayer was written by Dr. Percy Dearmer, a professor in the University of London. He was a prolific writer on all matters pertaining to liturgics, including the arts.

105. From A *Summarie of Devotions*. In plural form it is found in the American Prayer Book (p. 37), where much of the original flavor is lost.

106. Rev. Francis C. Lightbourn, S. T. M., is Librarian at the Seabury-Western Theological Seminary in Evanston, Ill. Many of his prayers

appeared first in *The Living Church,* of which he was Literary Editor, 1950-1963.

123. Slightly re-phrased to widen its application.

125. The inspiration for this prayer is a story told by Evelyn Underhill and others. A day-laborer in rural France stopped on his way home every day and knelt before the altar of the local church. One day the priest asked, "What do you say during these times?" "Nothing, Father; I just look up at Him, and He looks down at me."

127. One of very few prayers which reconcile the paradox of heaven: that it is a condition both of rest and of service.

129. Lancelot Andrewes (1555-1626) was Dean of Westminster, Bishop of Chichester, Ely, and Winchester in turn, and headed the list of clergy chosen by King James to revise the Bible.

131. Martin Luther (1483-1546), an Augustinian Friar at 22, before his death had become the great German religious reformer.

133. Rev. Cornelius Bishop Smith (1834-1913) was rector of St. James' Church, New York, 1867-1895. His very searching prayers for the clergy were posthumously printed in a pamphlet edited by Charles Lewis Slattery while rector of Grace Church, New York.

135. This prayer is found in many books, in a variety of wordings. In no case is the author named.

138. Dr. Samuel M. Shoemaker, rector of Calvary Church, New York (1925-1952), and of Calvary Church, Pittsburgh (1952 until his death in 1963), was a prolific writer, and a tireless advocate and practitioner of evangelism, which he held should be the work of both clergymen and laymen.

141. Professor Nash taught at the Episcopal Theological School in Cambridge, Mass., 1882-1912.

142. Rev. Sherman E. Johnson has been Dean of the Church Divinity School of the Pacific since 1951.

144. This excellent prayer, from the Draft Prayer Book of the Canadian Church (1955), was not retained in the final Book in 1959. What was formerly The Church of England in Canada (1955) is now The Anglican Church of Canada.

146. Thomas Aquinas (1225-1274), saint, philosopher, and theologian, did much to systematize Christian thought. Intellectually and spiritually he was of great stature, a controversial figure in his lifetime, as today. This remarkable prayer, the identity of whose translator is uncertain, was brought to the attention of the Editor by Professor Glanville Downey.

147. Professor Glanville Downey, a specialist in patristics and the early Church, including the Eastern liturgies, is professor of history and classics at Indiana University.

150. The writer skilfully recognizes Luke's authorship both of his Gospel and of the Book of Acts.

151. The translator, Professor Downey, notes that this Liturgy dates from about the fourth century and so cannot have been written by St.

James. Originating in Syria, it was superseded by others, especially that which bears the name St. John Chrysostom.

153. The second half of a prayer by an anonymous presbyter in the committee to revise the Prayer Book for the 1892 edition.

161. From the *Liturgy of St. Mark*, translated by Professor Glanville Downey; who notes that this Liturgy, originating in Egypt, is not earlier than the fourth century.

172. Based on the first stanza of William Bright's post-communion hymn, written in 1865. (No. 488 in the Episcopal Hymnal.)

173. Dr. James Martineau (1805-1900), English philosopher and preacher, was for 45 years Professor of Mental and Moral Philosophy and Political Economy in Manchester New College.

175. Rev. Rowland Williams (1817-1870) was a theologian and biblical scholar of the Church of England. This prayer, from *Psalms and Litanies*, appears in a weakened form in the current American Prayer Book, page 594.

176. Phillips Brooks (1835-1893), for many years rector of Trinity Church in Boston, Mass., where he achieved fame as a preacher, was made Bishop of Massachusetts shortly before his death.

177. Søren Kierkegaard (1813-1855), Danish philosopher and theologian, prolific writer, is generally regarded as the father of modern existentialism.

184. St. Anselm (1033-1109), Archbishop of Canterbury from 1093, quarrelled with two kings. His most famous work was a treatise on the Atonement, *Cur Deus Homo*.

187. Harry Emerson Fosdick, preacher, writer, counsellor, and teacher, for many years the Minister of Riverside Church in New York, put as much time and thought into the composition of a pastoral prayer as into the preparation of a sermon. "A public prayer," he writes, "should be an orderly sequence of collects." From certain prayers in his *A Book of Public Prayers* a few collects have been extracted, and used as such, in the present book.

189. The Latin version begins, "Excita, quaesumus, Domine" (Raise up, we beseech thee, O Lord), giving the prayer an appropriate burst of vigor at the start. Prayer 189 restores this feature.

194. The Prayer Book version (Cranmer's), as several people have pointed out, creates an ambiguity in the second clause by allowing the interpretation that we are asking God to put the armor of light on us. That this interpretation was not intended is made clear when one looks at the accompanying Epistle (page 91) and Romans 13:12. By a very slight change the ambiguity is dispelled.

196. The Prayer Book has "from the service of mammon." The final word in this phrase is difficult to pronounce so that it is heard correctly, and few who hear it correctly know what it means.

197. *Services For Broadcasting*, published by The British Broadcasting Corporation, was submitted to representatives of all the Christian denominations having any considerable following in England. The aim was to

appeal to the vast body of Christians who were willing to join with one another in an almost universal act of worship.

219. The changes in the wording avoid the redundant "of charity," and give a more personal sense of involvement at the end.

220. In the central petition this prayer reflects somewhat the translation of I Cor. 13 by J. B. Phillips. As to one's preference for *love* or *charity* as the name of the quality extolled by St. Paul, both are appropriate. Precisely what Paul means he spells out in verses 4-8.

224. Morgan Phelps Noyes, compiler and editor of *Prayers for Services,* has cast his net far and wide and drawn upon a great variety of sources, arranging the material with remarkable skill.

273. Bishop Scarlett's prayers are suffused with the single motive of service toward our neighbors—a motive which has characterized his self-giving life for over half a century.

278. After reading prayers of Roman and English background, with what Evelyn Underhill called their "austerity and economy of phrase," it is refreshing to come upon a prayer from Southern France in the eighth or ninth century, with its gaiety and fervor and warmth.

289. The late Msgr. Ronald Knox's version of Psalm 92 (93 in the King James and the Prayer Book numbering). Obviously this is an exception to the statement in Note 278.

296. Dr. Barclay's prayers combine beauty with realism. Calling things by their true names, he leaves the reader with the feeling that each prayer is expressly for him.

302. Professor Glanville Downey's translation from the Liturgy named for St. John Chrysostom, now the chief liturgy of the Orthodox Church. Sixth century. From a longer prayer used by the Priest at the beginning of the Eucharist.

309. A comparison of this prayer as proposed in 1952 with the final form adopted in 1961 illustrates once again a tendency common to all legislative bodies engaged in liturgical creativity. Prayer 309 is shorter than the one finally adopted. The latter adds a ponderous trinitarian ending, as long as all the rest of the prayer, which, though theologically impeccable, destroys the literary balance of the prayer as a whole, and in all probability causes the mind of the listener to wander from the theme of the prayer itself.

315. Based on Psalms 23, 103, and 150. Dated 1680. These are two of the four stanzas of a well-known hymn.

317. The committee appointed to prepare the 1892 edition of the American Prayer Book, in 1883 produced a complete book in draft form. This contained William Bright's prayer, with changes. In place of "from whom every good prayer cometh" they suggested "who hast bidden us seek that we may find." General Convention rejected the whole prayer. A later Convention, which adopted the current edition of 1928, admitted the prayer *minus* both of the clauses quoted above, thus shortening (and damaging) Bright's original. Prayer 317 stands as Bright wrote it.

320. Based on Hebrews 4:14-16, as translated by J. B. Phillips. The

clause "except that he never sinned" is a reminder that often we are tempted as the result of *having* sinned (tempted to sin again). This "experience of temptation" is one Jesus never encountered.

322. One of William Bright's best-known prayers, re-written by A. S. T. Fisher in what the latter called an adaptation so extensive as virtually to produce a new prayer. The original can be seen on page 595 of the American Prayer Book.

332. In prayer-construction a desirable feature is that of inner logic, or self-consistency, as when the author maintains from beginning to end a single metaphor, developing it from step to step and letting it unfold. This requires a disciplined mind and a lively imagination. Of such prayers John Donne was a master.

334. Two versions, one in *Daily Prayer* by Dean Milner-White and G. W. Briggs, the other in *A Collection of Prayers Used at Groton School,* have contributed to Prayer 334.

350. Seldom does one find on this side of the Atlantic the full text of Bishop Ridding's *A Litany of Remembrance.* The entire litany is here given in the belief that all of it is important. Its outstanding feature is the deeply probing insight which enabled the Bishop of Southwell to lay bare the temptations and weaknesses which all too often beset earnest men and women who carry the responsibilities of leadership in the Church. The slight changes in wording are intended to clarify certain expressions which by now seem dated, or to substitute American English for English English where the two differ.

352. Following the good example set by the finest collects in the Book of Common Prayer, "we" and "our" have been substituted for "they" and "their" in order to give the listeners a more vivid sense of personal involvement.

354. The Very Rev. E. S. Rousmaniere, while Dean of the Cathedral in Boston, Mass., conducted a Class in Personal Religion and edited a leaflet which in every issue contained this prayer, written by his friend Rev. Charles Morris Addison, a member of the Commission revising the Prayer Book for the 1928 edition.

358. One who had to endure great suffering wrote to a minister in a distant city, "By return post send me a prayer to use as Lent approaches." Written hurriedly in response, this prayer was sent, accompanied by the message, "Have a good Lent; not too subdued and Lentish, but joyful and full of peace."

380. Rev. Francis C. Lightbourn points out that in each of the Antiphons Christ is addressed by one of his Messianic titles, and that one or more of his mighty acts are named with each petition. A metrical version of the Antiphons is found in the hymn, "O come, O come, Emmanuel."

401. In many Anglican Prayer Books, beginning with the first (1549), the office called The Visitation of the Sick contained at least one short sermon (called the Exhortation) addressed to the sick person. It was Dr. William Reed Huntington who saw the possibility of taking a sentence

from one of these Exhortations and joining it to another of about the same length to form a collect. Thus he made a cento, a literary work made of parts of other compositions. He delighted in doing this, and put his talent to good use many a time. Another Huntington cento is the collect for the Transfiguration, in the American Prayer Book on page 247.

414. Rev. Frederic Palmer (1848-1932), rector of Christ Church in Andover, Mass., 1888-1913, wrote six books dealing with the controversial theological problems of his day, in which he combined a liberal outlook with intense devotion to Jesus Christ as Master.

415. In 1951 the Church of India, Pakistan, Burma, and Ceylon included this magnificent Dismissal in its Proposed Prayer Book. Its title is "The Christaraksha: to be said by the Priest." (The key word, unfamiliar to Western ears, means "Christ our Protector.") The final edition, of 1961, rejected it—reminding us of the editorial perils described in Note 317, and perhaps suggesting that East and West are not so far apart after all.

424. Compare the hymn, "Come down, O Love Divine," translated from the Italian by Richard F. Littledale. The author, Bianco da Siena, who lived during the 14th century, may have provided Bishop Brent with the inspiration for this prayer.

425-430. These affirmations from individuals have the value of sincerity and simplicity and depth.

431. Some have thought that this prayer was written by Lena Sorabji, daughter of the first Parsee in India to become a Christian. A copy of it, with changes, was found among her effects. But the Editor has seen no evidence that would cast doubt on the Rankin authorship. Moreover, those who name Miss Sorabji as author refer to the prayer as an intercession, which it has never been, for it is always couched in the first-person plural.

433. The translator, Professor Glanville Downey, notes that in the Eastern Orthodox Church this Liturgy is used on Wednesdays and Fridays during Lent, and on the first three days of Holy Week. Communion is made with consecrated Bread and Wine reserved from a previous day.

440. Even a cursory reading of the prayers and meditations by the late Rev. Samuel S. Drury will establish him as a deeply religious man with a strikingly original vocabulary and an independent point-of-view.

442. At the end of his *The Sense of the Presence Of God*, the Gifford Lectures of 1961-1962, Professor John Baillie quotes this prayer by "the last of our Caroline poets."

446. Rev. Russell L. Dicks, in partnership with the late Richard C. Cabot, M. D., has practised the art of ministering to the sick for over thirty years, taking careful notes along the way, growing in insight and power, and bringing to hundreds of patients a depth of faith and of self-understanding which transfigures suffering and overcomes, in Christ's Name, the fear of death.

449. Most parents pray *for* their sick child. To pray also *with* him can be of enormous help both to the child and to the parents, for it lays before

God the predicament all three are in, and cements the family's unity in love.

457. Dr. Weatherhead has the ability to describe a human situation so vividly that we are sure he knows what he is talking about. In all intercessions this is a priceless gift. It is especially valuable when spoken in the presence of the sufferer, who is then likely to say to himself, "This man understands."

459. The first sentence has been in Anglican Prayer Books since 1549, thanks to Cranmer. (American Prayer Book, page 332.) Professor Massey Shepherd in his Commentary says that its author was a monk named Notker, who lived in Switzerland in the ninth century. It expresses the medieval sense of awe and dread in the presence of death—a feeling which more and more people are coming to see has its proper place, and need not be elaborately disguised.

460. Based on the well-known Communion Hymn, "Bread of the World" (pub. 1827) by Reginald Heber (1783-1826), who won fame as a hymn-writer, and toward the end of his short life became Bishop of Calcutta.

475. Professor Massey Shepherd points out that this is the final paragraph of the prayer for the Church in the Scottish Book of 1637.

Sources

OFFICIAL PRAYER BOOKS

Following the name of the Prayer Book, and the reference to its publisher or publishers, and date of publication, the first numeral identifies the prayer in this compilation. The second numeral, in parenthesis, indicates on what page the prayer can be found in the book used by the Editor. This does not mean that basically the same prayer is not to be found in many other books, both official and unofficial. Several prayers have been modified, as can be seen by consulting the book the Editor used.

The Book of Common Prayer of the Protestant Episcopal Church in the United States of America. Edition of 1928-1929. Printed and distributed by several publishers in the United States, with uniform pagination. Certified by the Custodian of the Standard Book (master copy). Not copyrighted. 4 (44); 44 (44); 58 (18); 59 (35); 67 (194); 94 (49); 109 (590); 123 (595); 124 (42); 148 (92); 165 (83); 178 (49); 180 (67); 183 (197); 189 (95); 190 (49); 192 (174); 194 (90); 196 (44); 211 (598); 215 (596); 219 (122); 224 (599); 234 (109); 271 (99); 312 (596); 334 (62); 345 (588); 352 (218); 359 (595); 367 (588); 375 (591); 378 (31); 400 (147); 443 (253); 469 (268); 475 (336).

The Book of Common Prayer of the Church of India, Pakistan, Burma, and Ceylon. The Indian Society for Promoting Christian Knowledge, Madras, 1961. 33 (623); 128 (49).

The Book of Common Prayer of the Anglican Church of Canada. Cambridge University Press, Toronto, 1959. 205 (731); 294 (736); 394 (115).

A Book of Common Prayer of the Church of the Province of South Africa. Oxford University Press, London: Cape Town, 1960. 380 (20); 462 (709).

The Book of Common Worship of The Church of South India. Oxford University Press, Madras, 1963. 132 (66).

The Book of Common Worship of the Presbyterian Church in the United States of America. Board of Christian Education of the Presbyterian Church in the U.S.A., Philadelphia, 1946. 39 (328).

Collects and Prayers, The United Lutheran Church in America. The Board of Publication of The United Lutheran Church in America, Philadelphia, 1935. 107 (209); 410 (170).

The Book of Common Order of the Church of Scotland. Oxford, London, 1957. 55 (295); 65 (277); 70 (27); 179 (47); 222 (273); 267 (278); 468 (165).

Prayers for the Christian Year, Church of Scotland. Oxford, London, 1957.
397 (58); 398 (59); 421 (128).
The Book of Common Prayer, The Church of Ireland. A.P.C.K., Dublin,
1960. 68 (28); 130 (35); 455 (276); 470 (29).
Services for Broadcasting, British Broadcasting Corp., London, 1931.
197 (62); 262 (25); 314 (28); 386 (4).

PROPOSED PRAYER BOOKS

From time to time special committees of various Christian
Churches have drawn up proposals for revising their respective Prayer
Books, using such titles as *Proposed Revisions* (Methodist), *Additions and
Deviations* (Church of England), *Draft Prayer Book* (Canada), *Proposed
Prayer Book* (India, Pakistan, Burma, Ceylon), *The Book Annexed*
(Episcopal, USA).

Such publications enable the governing body of a Church to consider
a suggested new Prayer Book as a whole, instead of piece-meal: a great
advantage, since changes in one part of a book affect, or are affected by,
changes in another part.

In every proposed book a number of items fail to receive the votes
required for acceptance in the final revision, though some of the rejected
material may have great merit. To rescue a few of these becomes the
privilege of non-official compilations; and, more rarely, of official ones also,
as when a later revision-committee reverses (in part) the action of its
predecessor.

The Book Annexed, adopted by the General Convention in 1883, Prot-
estant Episcopal Church (USA). 36 (65); 81 (50); 82 (50);
153 (151).
*The Book of Common Prayer with the Additions and Deviations Proposed
in 1928*, Church of England. Oxford University Press. 388 (174).
Draft Report of the Joint Committee, 1955, Church of England in Canada.
Cambridge University Press. 19 (57); 145 (46).
A *Proposed Prayer Book*, authorized by the Episcopal Synod in 1951,
Church of India, Pakistan, Burma, and Ceylon. Diocesan Press, Madras.
309 (63); 415 (57).

PROPOSED OPTIONAL ADDITIONS

In addition to over-all revision is the issue of a smaller booklet pre-
senting proposed new material on one particular subject, for trial use under
certain restrictions.

Prayer Book Studies XVI was put in print by the Church Pension Fund
of the Episcopal Church (USA), at the request of the Standing Liturgical Commission, in 1963. 101 (90); 134 (79); 146 (88).
A *Plea* for a distinctive Liturgy for the Indian Church. With a suggested
Form. Edited by J. C. Winslow. Preface by the Right Rev. E. J.
Palmer, Bishop of Bombay. Recommended by him to be allowed for
experimental use. Longmans, Green, & Co., Bombay, 1920. 311 (92).

OTHER SOURCES

This list does not refer to anthologies other than the one used by the Editor. The initial source of many prayers cannot be traced.

Baillie, John, *A Diary of Private Prayer*, Scribners, N. Y., 1949. 1 (67); 73 (39); 207 (55); 214 (89); 285 (103); 310 (125); 330 (15); 454 (113).

Barclay, William, *A Book of Everyday Prayers*, Harpers, N. Y., 1959. 296 (34); 337 (76); 393 (106).

Binyon, Gilbert Clive, *Prayers for the City of God*, Longmans, London, 1927. 28 (136); 251 (12); 254 (23).

Bright, William, Translations by, *Ancient Collects*, Parker, London, 1908. 95 (98); 99 (100); 108 (81); 318 (2).

Bright, William, Originals, *Ancient Collects*, Parker, London, 1908. 82 (238); 123 (233); 136 (235); 172 (based on his post-communion hymn); 182 (234); 317 (233); 322 (234) revised by A. S. T. Fisher in his *Anthology of Prayers*, p. 56.

Brooke, Avery, *Youth Talks with God*, Scribners, N. Y., 1959. 204 (37); 232 (25); 242 (17); 257 (50); 333 (41).

Dicks, Russell L. (with R. C. Cabot), *The Art of Ministering to the Sick*, Macmillan, N. Y., 1961. 446 (225); 454 (224).

Drury, S. S., *Draw Near With Faith*, Harpers, N. Y., 1936. 411 (47); 440 (163).

"E. W.", *A Book of Simple Prayers*, Reading, England, 1893. 213 (98); 250 (38) by George Dawson; 295 (49) by E. W.; 381 (92) by E. W.; 435 (22) by George Dawson.

Ferris, Theodore P., *Book of Prayer for Everyman*, Seabury, N. Y., 1962. 244 (127); 366 (1); 436 (7); 447 (129); 450 (126).

Fisher, A. S. T., *An Anthology of Prayers*, Longmans, N. Y., 1943. 83 (43); 159 (76); 279 (40); 282 (13); 293 (41); 369 (59).

Fosbroke, H. E. W., *By Means Of Death*, Seabury, N. Y., 1956. 404 (26); 405 (33); 406 (51); 407 (58); 408 (73); 409 (82).

Fosdick, Harry Emerson, *A Book of Public Prayers*, Harpers, N. Y., 1959. 187 (94); 263 (13); 345 (12).

Fox, George, *A Day-Book of Counsel and Comfort*, Macmillan, London, 1937. 62 (18); 191 (200); 300 (112); 355 (182).

Grant, Frederick C., *Christ's Victory and Ours*, Macmillan, N. Y., 1950. 34 (67); 72 (48); 122 (36); 343 (19).

The Grey Book, American Ed. Oxford University Press, N. Y., 1958. 25 (46); 42 (75); 49 (83); 60 (84); 63 (79); 88 (74); 102 (27-29); 104 (33); 114 (72); 135 (80); 158 (73); 181 (70); 195 (34); 227 (55); 231 (7); 261 (71); 272 (15-16); 290 (25); 299 (38); 313 (25); 377 (78-79); 462 (85); 480 (61).

Hoyland, J. S., *A Book of Prayers Written for Use in an Indian College*, The Challenge Book & Pictures, London, 1926. 297 (119).

Hunter, John, *Devotional Services for Public Worship*, Dent, London, 1903. 92 (135); 119 (270); 306 (119); 396 (227).

Kierkegaard, Søren, *The Prayers of Kierkegaard*, Chicago University Press, 1956. 177 (67); 340 (37).

Manschreck, Clyde, *Prayers of the Reformers*, Fortress Press, Philadelphia, 1958. 53 (103); 80 (102); 112 (63); 131 (108); 166 (47); 206 (77).

Martineau, James, *Home Prayers*, London, 1900. 173 (132); 186 (85); 372 (138); 434 (88).

McComb, Samuel, *A Book of Prayers*, Dodd, Mead, N. Y., 1912. 79 (191); 139 (207); 284 (68); 292 (109); 327 (51); 439 (187); 451 (53); 461 (169).

Merton, Thomas, *A Thomas Merton Reader*, Harcourt, Brace & World, N. Y. 1961. 3 (303); 288 (343).

Miller, Samuel H., *Prayers for Daily Use*, Harpers, N. Y., 1957. 162 (108); 185 (7); 226 (104); 464 (115).

Milner-White, Eric, *After the Third Collect*, Mowbray, London, 1952. 13 (11); 103 (12).

Milner-White, Eric, and Briggs, G. W., *Daily Prayer*, Oxford, London, 1946. 12 (96); 199 (10); 229 (24); 252 (11); 274 (95); 319 (55).

Niebuhr, Reinhold, *A Litany for All Workers*, Crowell, N. Y. (in *With One Voice*, compiled by R. M. Bartlett). 1961. 91 (142).

Noyes, Morgan Phelps, *Prayers for Services*, Scribners, N. Y., 1934. 224 (106); 283 (79).

Rodenmayer, Robert N., *The Pastor's Prayerbook*, Oxford, N. Y., 1960. 78 (91); 84 (117); 142 (65); 212 (96); 238 (244); 445 (119).

Scarlett, William, *To Will One Thing*, Privately printed, St. Louis, 1948. 30 (11); 31 (10); 48 (57); 203 (manuscript); 273 (54); 291 (18); 361 (94).

Soulsby, L. H. M., *The Old World and the New*, Longmans, London, 1922. 198 (39); 208 (40); 235 (39); 239 (38); 242 (2).

Stephens, John U., *Prayers of the Christian Life*, Oxford, N. Y., 1952. 96 (74); 249 (147); 324 (73); 374 (46).

Suter, John Wallace, *Prayers of the Spirit*, Harpers, N. Y., 1943. 6 (36); 8 (41); 14 (36); 24 (18); 26 (42); 37 (34); 50 (7); 52 (35); 57 (35); 61 (41); 76 (42); 90 (30); 93 (49); 113 (7); 121 (2); 170 (5); 200 (11); 236 (8); 323 (9); 376 (1); 382 (18); 390 (19); 399 (22); 402 (10); 413 (23); 416 (24); 442 (15); 446 (27); 450 (27); 456 (28); 458 (27); 461 (26); 465 (29); 475 (32); 489 (33).

Suter, John Wallace, *A Book of Collects* (by "Pater and Filius"), Morehouse, Milwaukee, 1919. 14 (14); 52 (15); 75 (33); 240 (8); 243 (35); 385 (14).

Weatherhead, Leslie D., *A Private House of Prayer*, Abingdon, N. Y., 1958. 17 (226); 457 (69).

Wolf, William J., *The Religion of Abraham Lincoln*, Seabury, N. Y., 1964. 430 (195).

Index of First Lines

The number after each line refers to the prayer number.

Index of Authors